ONE POT

RECIPES

ONE POT
RECIPES

Meals for Your Slow Cooker, Pressure Cooker,
Dutch Oven, Sheet Pan, Skillet, and More

Ellen BROWN

STERLING EPICURE
New York

STERLING EPICURE
New York

An Imprint of Sterling Publishing Co., Inc.
1166 Avenue of the Americas
New York, NY 10036

ISBN 978-1-4549-2923-9

Distributed in Canada by Sterling Publishing Co., Inc.
c/o Canadian Manda Group, 664 Annette Street
Toronto M6S 2C8, Ontario, Canada
Distributed in the United Kingdom by GMC Distribution Services
Castle Place, 166 High Street, Lewes, East Sussex BN7 1XU, England
Distributed in Australia by NewSouth Books
45 Beach Street, Coogee, NSW 2034, Australia

For information about custom editions, special sales, and
premium and corporate purchases, please contact Sterling Special Sales
at 800-805-5489 or specialsales@sterlingpublishing.com.

Manufactured in China

2 4 6 8 10 9 7 5 3 1

www.sterlingpublishing.com

Cover design by Jo Obarowski
Photography by Bill Milne
Food styling by Diane Vezza

contents

INTRODUCTION

Benjamin Franklin wrote, "Nothing can be said to be certain, except death and taxes." But I'd like to add a third item to that list. It's equally certain that no one loves scrubbing pots and pans. Aphorisms become so because they're true. Scrubbing up after a dinner is right up there on the list of dreaded events with having a root canal without Novocain.

That's why this book was born. It offers you maximum flavor with minimal cleanup. Whenever possible the one pot or pan you use for assembling your entire dinner is covered in foil. That reduces post-dinner puttering to crumbling up a sheet of dirty aluminum foil and scoring a two-pointer tossing it into the garbage can.

If the recipe calls for cooking on top of your stove, all you need is one burner; you could successfully make these dishes on a hot plate. Other recipes start on the stovetop but are then completed with unattended cooking time in the oven, and then there are those that roast or bake while you read a book.

I have written more than forty cookbooks, but this is the first in which the recipes are divided by the one piece of cooking equipment that is needed to prepare the food rather than by the ingredients. Instead of chapters titled "Poultry" or "Meat," you'll find "Slow Cookers" and "Sheet Pans."

Cooking with just one pot or a pan is a welcome throwback to the historic roots of American cooking. It's only been in the past century that cooking has involved *more* than a few pans. That's because most folks only had one pot and one skillet, and those were probably inherited from a relative, rather than purchased new. If a meal didn't get cooked in a Dutch oven or a cast iron skillet, it probably didn't get made at all.

Using different and specialized pans for home cooking can be traced to the mid-twentieth century, when European restaurant cooking was in vogue. French chefs had scores of scrubbing hands at their disposal, so using a baker's dozen of baking sheets and sauté pans to make one dish was never questioned.

One of my favorite examples of this is a traditional recipe for ratatouille, in which each vegetable was cooked individually and then combined with the others at the end. My version, which you'll find on page 184, and which includes an herbed pork tenderloin for protein, is baked on a sheet pan, and the vegetables are added to the pan sequentially, so all the ingredients reach the finish line at the same time.

Each recipe in this book gives you a complete and balanced meal that includes a protein, vegetables, and, most of the time, a starch or legume, so you don't have to make more than one recipe for dinner. There's no flipping back and forth in the book to see if the flavor of the side dishes you've selected will be harmonious with the entrée. There's no guesswork involved, and everything is ready simultaneously, because the entire meal is prepared in one pan or pot.

Both old and new concepts underlie many of these dishes. For example, in Chapter 6, which is devoted to cooking on sheet pans, you'll find methods that go back to classic French cuisine, such as en papillote, which involves steaming a dish in a paper or aluminum foil pouch. Other recipes in the book would enrage the most classic Italian cooks, such as a dish in which the pasta is actually cooked in the sauce. The result? Pasta that really tastes better, because it has inherent flavor, rather than merely serving as a base carrier for a topping.

In addition to five chapters that feature everyday pots and pans, two focus on electric appliances. One is the slow cooker, which you can now find in just about as many kitchens as the coffee pot; both have a household penetration of more than 90 percent. The slow cooker is modeled after the antique bean pot, which was nestled into the embers of the fire to cook beans overnight. The modern electric slow cooker first gained fame in the early 1970s when women entered the workforce in large numbers.

The other appliance is a lightning-speed version of the slow cooker, an electric pressure cooker best known as the Instant Pot®. In Chapter 1 I give directions for both electric and stovetop pressure cookers, because, as a Pleistocene Person, I still like the ability to control the level of heat by turning a knob on my gas range. Stovetop models have been improved with myriad safety features during the past decade, so there should be less anxiety when using them.

So venture forth to join the ranks of those of us released from the tedium of cleaning up. Regardless of your age or cooking abilities, you'll never have to scrub more than one pot when you cook from this book.

Happy cooking!

Ellen Brown

Providence, Rhode Island

chapter 1

Instant Pots and Pressure Cookers

No appliance has undergone a renaissance like the pressure cooker, especially Instant Pot®, the latest electric version. While pressure cooking as a method was introduced in the seventeenth century, it wasn't until the twenty-first century that a machine was devised to deliver the primary benefit of literally cooking under pressure: getting a nutritious meal on the table in a matter of just a few minutes.

In the United States busy women adopted the pressure cooker in droves during World War II, when so many of them worked outside the home, and almost half of all homes in the 1950s used a pressure cooker on a regular basis. But this number plummeted as postwar cooks looked to the convenience of frozen foods that were reheated in the oven or, later, "nuked" in a microwave.

While electric pressure cookers were patented in 1991, it was the 2009 introduction of the Instant Pot that did for pressure cookers what Crock-Pot® did for slow cookers. The new generation of pressure cookers is totally user-friendly, with tons of built-in safety mechanisms; the most important of which ensures that the pressure cooker will not turn on unless the lid is properly secured. Sales soared because cooks trusted the electric pot, and even stovetop models are regaining favor.

The father of the pressure cooker was a French physicist Denis Papin, who made his reputation in the 1670s for his studies of steam and how to best use it. While working in London a few years later in the early 1680s, he prepared a whole meal for members of the Royal Society to show how food could be cooked much faster if the boiling point of water is raised by trapping its steam in a tightly closed pot.

How Pressure Cookers Work

The low temperature at which water boils (212°F/100°C) in an uncovered pot keeps cooking in the slow lane, as steam escapes into the open air. But when you lock the lid on a specially designed pressure cooker, you are in effect converting an open space into a closed space. As the steam can no longer escape, pressure builds up and the temperature of the water rises. This is called the PSI, an abbreviation for *pounds per square inch*.

So why does the temperature of the water increase above the boiling point? As heat is applied to any liquid, its constituent molecules move more rapidly and move farther apart. When a liquid boils, it changes state: that is, a portion of the liquid vaporizes. For water, this means that steam is produced at 212°F (100°C). In a pot that is open to the air, steam escapes into the atmosphere. But if the pot is tightly closed, the transformation of water into steam is delayed because the increased pressure of the steam delays vaporization. As more and more heat is applied to the pot, the water temperature rises, and the trapped steam pressure rises above atmospheric pressure.

There are tables that can tell you what the water temperature is for various steam pressures. Most modern pressure cookers are set to run at 15 psi. The corresponding water temperature is about 250°F (120°C). When these heat/pressure relationships for cooking are used, the heat under the pot is reduced once the desired pressure (and corresponding temperature) is reached.

So what pressure cookers do on the cooking superhighway is to raise the speed limit. It's not just the water molecules around the food that heat up far beyond the 212°F (100°C), it's also the water molecules *inside* the food. That's why cuts of meat reach an ethereal state of meltingly tender so quickly when they're cooked under pressure. The water molecules inside the meat are not strolling along at 212°F (100°C); they are jogging to the finish line at 250°F (120°C).

The general rule is that for every 41°F (5°C) that the boiling point of water is increased, the cooking time is cut in half. So a stew that would take 3 hours of conventional simmering will be pressure-cooked to perfection in 20 minutes.

Pressure Cooking Savvy

The most important thing you can do is to *read the instruction manual for your pressure cooker from cover to cover.* I cannot stress this enough. While a particular kind of blender may have a unique combination of bells and whistles, *all* blenders are pretty much the same. The same cannot be said about pressure cookers; they even vary as to the pressure level they reach. The Instant Pot, for example, takes longer to cook food than a stovetop pressure cooker because it only reaches 12 psi rather than the 15 psi of conventional cookers.

Next to reading the instruction manual, the key to success when using a pressure cooker is to *release the pressure using the method specified in the recipe.* Keep in mind that the food is cooking both before and after the pressure cooker reaches pressure. In order to start forming pressure, the liquid must reach the temperature of boiling, and it will remain at that temperature for a variable time after the official cooking time is over.

There are only a few options for how to release the pressure, so it's not a difficult subject to master, and if you're not following a specific recipe, my advice is to consult a similar recipe to determine both the duration for cooking under pressure and the suggested release method.

Natural release: *This couldn't be easier. Turn off the heat source and wait until the pot's safety features unlock or give you the signal that it's safe to open the pot. For a gas stove, turning off the burner is all you need to do, and for an electric or halogen stove, turn off the burner, slide the pot onto a cool burner,* and let it rest there. If you're using an electric cooker, unplug it from the wall so that it doesn't automatically go into its "keep warm" mode.

Timed natural release: *One variation of natural release is that occasionally you're instructed to use it for a finite amount of time and then quick-release any pressure that remains. The most common variable is a 10-minute natural release, so when you remove the cooker from the heat source, or unplug it, you set your timer again.*

Quick release: *This is the method to use for foods that cook relatively fast to prevent overcooking. The important thing to remember is to point the steam valve away from you, because when you open it the steam will come out with a lot of force. During the winter it's nice to get some humidity in the house, but in warm months I frequently place the cooker on a table in front of an open window.*

Stovetop Pressure Cooker

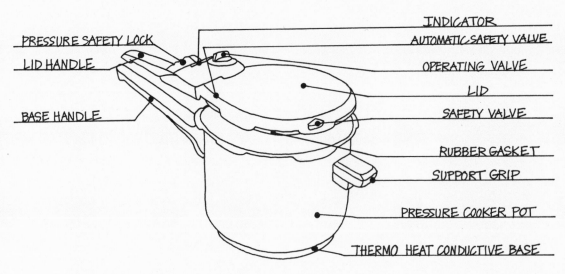

PRESSURE SAFETY LOCK
LID HANDLE
BASE HANDLE

INDICATOR
AUTOMATIC SAFETY VALVE
OPERATING VALVE
LID
SAFETY VALVE
RUBBER GASKET
SUPPORT GRIP
PRESSURE COOKER POT
THERMO HEAT CONDUCTIVE BASE

Electric Pressure Cooker

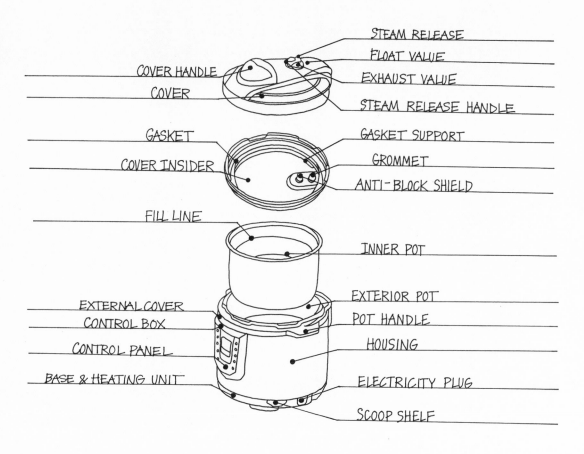

STEAM RELEASE

FLOAT VALUE

COVER HANDLE

EXHAUST VALUE

COVER

STEAM RELEASE HANDLE

GASKET

GASKET SUPPORT

COVER INSIDER

GROMMET

ANTI-BLOCK SHIELD

FILL LINE

INNER POT

EXTERIOR POT

EXTERNAL COVER

POT HANDLE

CONTROL BOX

CONTROL PANEL

HOUSING

BASE & HEATING UNIT

ELECTRICITY PLUG

SCOOP SHELF

Vegetarian Black Bean Chili

Here's a hearty chili that—except for the garnishes—is totally vegan. The combination of smoked Spanish paprika and chipotle chiles adds a smoky nuance to its flavor.

SERVES **4 to 6**

SIZE **6-quart or larger pressure cooker**

TIME **6 to 8 minutes at high pressure with natural pressure release for 15 minutes**

The reason to make sure the soaked beans are coated with oil before the liquid is added is to keep them from creating foam as they cook.

1 pound dried black beans, soaked
¼ cup olive oil, divided
2 red bell peppers, seeds and ribs removed, diced
1 large red onion, diced
4 garlic cloves, minced
2 tablespoons chili powder
1 tablespoon smoked Spanish paprika
1 tablespoon ground cumin
2 chipotle chiles in adobo sauce, finely chopped
3 cups Vegetable Stock (page 33) or store-bought stock

3 tablespoons tomato paste
1 cup fresh corn kernels
¼ cup chopped fresh cilantro
Salt and freshly ground black pepper, to taste
Tortilla chips, for serving
Sour cream, for serving
Shredded cheddar cheese, for serving
Lime wedges, for serving

Rinse the beans in a colander and place them in a mixing bowl covered with cold salted water. Allow the beans to soak for a minimum of 6 hours or overnight. Or place the beans in a saucepan of salted water and bring them to a boil over high heat. Boil for 1 minute. Turn off the heat, cover the pan, and soak the beans for 1 hour. Drain the beans, discard the soaking water, rinse the beans well, and cook or refrigerate them as soon as possible.

Heat 2 tablespoons of the oil in the Instant Pot using the browning function or over medium-high heat in a stovetop cooker. Add the red bell peppers and onion and cook, stirring frequently, for 2 minutes. Add the garlic and stir for 1 minute, or until the onion is translucent. Stir in the chili powder, paprika, and cumin, and cook for 30 seconds, stirring constantly.

Add the remaining oil and the beans to the cooker and stir the mixture well to coat the beans. Add the chipotle chiles and stock to the cooker, and stir well.

Close and lock the lid of the cooker.

NOTE The chili can be prepared up to 2 days in advance and refrigerated, tightly covered. Reheat it over low heat, covered, until hot.

ELECTRIC: Set the Instant Pot to cook at high pressure for 8 minutes. After 8 minutes, unplug the pot so it does not go into warming mode. Allow the pressure to return to normal naturally for 15 minutes. Quick release any remaining pressure. Remove the lid, tilting it away from you, to allow steam to escape.

OR

STOVETOP: Place the cooker over high heat and bring it to high pressure. Once high pressure is reached, reduce the heat as much as possible while retaining the high pressure level. Cook for 6 minutes. Take the pot off the heat and allow it to return to normal pressure naturally for 15 minutes. Quick release any remaining pressure. Remove the lid, tilting it away from you, to allow steam to escape.

Stir the tomato paste, corn, and cilantro into the chili and cook for 3 minutes using the browning function of the Instant Pot or over medium-high heat. Season with salt and pepper.

To serve, ladle the chili into bowls and pass the tortilla chips, sour cream, cheese, and lime wedges around the table separately.

Summer Corn Risotto

The sweetness of fresh corn is amplified by the equally sweet red bell pepper in this easy-to-make vegetarian dish. Serve it with a tossed salad in a lemony vinaigrette dressing and enjoy any leftovers as a salad the next day with some of the same dressing.

SERVES **4 to 6**

SIZE **4-quart or larger pressure cooker**

> To prove to yourself how much sweet corn flavor is found in the corncobs, taste the risotto before adding the kernels. What you'll find is that the cobs have already made the dish taste like corn. That's why I always add them to corn chowders as they simmer, too.

3 ears fresh corn, shucked
3 tablespoons unsalted butter
2 leeks, white and pale green parts, sliced and rinsed well
½ red bell pepper, seeds and ribs removed, diced
2 garlic cloves, minced
1½ cups Arborio rice

½ cup dry white wine
4 cups Vegetable Stock (page 32), Chicken Stock (page 30), or store-bought stock, divided
Salt and freshly ground black pepper, to taste
½ cup freshly grated Parmesan cheese

Cut the kernels off the corn and set aside. Reserve the cobs.

Melt the butter in the Instant Pot using the browning function or over medium heat in a stovetop cooker. Add the leeks and red bell pepper and cook, stirring occasionally, for 2 minutes. Add the garlic and cook for 1 minute, or until the leeks are translucent. Stir in the rice and cook, stirring constantly, for 2 minutes. Stir in the wine and cook for 1 minute, or until the wine is almost evaporated. Stir in 3½ cups of the stock and the corncobs.

Close and lock the lid of the cooker.

ELECTRIC: Set the Instant Pot to cook at high pressure for 8 minutes. After 8 minutes, unplug the pot so that it does not go into warming mode. Quick release the pressure according to the method provided by the manufacturer. Remove the lid, tilting it away from you, to allow steam to escape.

OR

STOVETOP: Place the cooker over high heat and bring it to high pressure. Once high pressure is reached, reduce the heat as much as possible while still retaining the high pressure level. Cook for 7 minutes. Quick release the pressure according to the method provided by the manufacturer. Remove the lid, tilting it away from you, to allow steam to escape.

NOTE Risotto should be cooked just prior to serving.

Remove and discard the corncobs from the cooker. Continue to cook the risotto using the browning function of the Instant Pot or over medium heat for 3 minutes, stirring constantly, or until the liquid has thickened. Stir in the corn kernels, and cook for an additional 2 minutes. Add some of the remaining stock if needed to achieve the proper creamy consistency. Season with salt and pepper, and serve immediately, passing the cheese separately.

Salmon and Rice Pilaf
with Chimichurri Sauce

While chimichurri sauce is used most often on beef in its native Argentina,
I love how its fresh taste enlivens a meaty, oily fish like salmon. The rice
is cooked in seafood stock and also benefits from a dab of sauce.

SERVES **4 to 6**

SIZE **6-quart or larger pressure cooker**

TIME **3 to 4 minutes at high pressure with 10 minute natural pressure release**

A vegetable peeler and a pair of tweezers are the best ways to get rid of those pesky little bones in fish fillets and steaks. Run a peeler down the center of the fillet, starting at the tail end. It will catch the larger pin bones, and with a twist of your wrist, you can pull them out. For finer bones, use your fingers to rub the flesh lightly and then pull out the bones with the tweezers.

SALMON AND RICE

1½ cups basmati rice
2 tablespoons olive oil
2 shallots, minced
1 carrot, diced
¼ red bell pepper, seeds and ribs removed, diced
¾ cups Seafood Stock (page 32) or store-bought stock
¼ cup dry white wine
2 tablespoons freshly squeezed lemon juice
2 tablespoons chopped fresh parsley
2 teaspoons fresh thyme leaves
Salt and freshly ground black pepper, to taste
4 to 6 (6-ounce) salmon steaks, 1½-inches thick

2 tablespoons unsalted butter, melted and cooled
½ lemon, thinly sliced with seeds discarded

SAUCE

1 cup firmly packed fresh parsley leaves
3 garlic cloves, peeled
2 tablespoons fresh oregano leaves
2 tablespoons freshly squeezed lemon juice
Salt, to taste
¼ teaspoon crushed red pepper flakes, or to taste
½ cup olive oil

Place the rice in a sieve and rinse it under cold running water for 1 to 2 minutes, or until the water runs clear. Shake it in the sieve to get off as much moisture as possible.

Heat the oil in the Instant Pot using the browning function or over medium-high heat in a stovetop cooker. Add the shallots, carrot, and red bell pepper and cook, stirring frequently, for 3 minutes, or until the shallots are translucent. Add the rice, stock, wine, lemon juice, parsley, and thyme. Stir well and season with salt and pepper.

Brush both sides of the salmon with the melted butter and sprinkle with salt and pepper. Arrange the salmon in a steamer basket and lay the lemon slices on top of the fish. Place the steamer basket into the cooker on top of the rice mixture.

Close and lock the lid of the cooker.

ELECTRIC: Set the Instant Pot to cook at high pressure for 4 minutes. After 4 minutes, unplug the pot so it does not go into warming mode. Allow the pressure to return to normal naturally for 10 minutes. Quick release any remaining pressure. Remove the lid, tilting it away from you, to allow steam to escape.

OR

STOVETOP: Place the cooker over high heat and bring it to high pressure. Once high pressure is reached, reduce the heat as much as possible while still retaining the high pressure level. Cook for 3 minutes. Take the pot off the heat and allow it to return to normal pressure naturally for 10 minutes. Quick release any remaining pressure. Remove the lid, tilting it away from you, to allow steam to escape.

While the cooker builds pressure, make the sauce. Combine the parsley, garlic, and oregano in a food processor fitted with the steel blade and chop finely using on-and-off pulsing. Scrape the mixture into a mixing bowl and add the lemon juice, salt, and crushed red pepper flakes. Whisk in the olive oil, and set aside.

Gently lift the steamer basket out of the cooker and fluff the rice with a fork. To serve, place some of the rice on a plate and top it with a portion of salmon. Pass around the sauce separately, and serve immediately.

NOTE The rice can be prepared up to 2 days in advance and refrigerated, tightly covered. Reheat it over low heat or in a 300°F oven until hot.

VARIATION

* **Substitute halibut or cod** for the salmon; the cooking time will remain the same.

Red Bean Stew
with Chicken and Sausage

*Here's a hearty dish straight from the bayous of Louisiana that can be personalized to suit your
taste and preferred level of spice. The more hot red pepper sauce you add, the spicier it will be,
and you can always substitute a mild smoked sausage like kielbasa for the fiery Andouille.*

SERVES **4 to 6**

SIZE **6-quart or larger pressure cooker**

TIME **6 to 8 minutes at high pressure with natural pressure release for 15 minutes**

While Andouille originated in France, it was actually introduced to Louisiana by German immigrants in the eighteenth century. It's a coarsely textured sausage made with pork, garlic, pepper, onions, and wine. There are now many poultry versions on the market, too.

1 **pound dried red beans**
3 **tablespoons olive oil, divided**
4 to 6 **(4-ounce) boneless, skinless chicken thighs**
½ **pound Andouille pork or poultry sausage, cut into ¾-inch slices**
1 **large sweet onion, such as Vidalia or Bermuda, halved and sliced**
½ **red bell pepper, seeds and ribs removed, diced**

1 **celery rib, diced**
3 **garlic cloves, minced**
2½ **cups Chicken Stock (page 30) or store-bought stock**
2 **bay leaves**
¼ **cup chopped fresh parsley**
1 **tablespoon fresh thyme leaves**
Salt, to taste
Hot red pepper sauce, to taste

Rinse the beans in a colander and place them in a mixing bowl covered with cold salted water. Allow the beans to soak for a minimum of 6 hours or overnight. Or place the beans into a saucepan of salted water and bring to a boil over high heat. Boil 1 minute. Turn off the heat, cover the pan, and soak the beans for 1 hour. With either soaking method, drain the beans, discard the soaking water, rinse them well, and cook or refrigerate the beans as soon as possible.

Heat 2 tablespoons of the oil in the Instant Pot using the browning function or over medium-high heat in a stovetop cooker. Add the chicken and sausage and cook, turning the meats with tongs, until browned. Remove the meats from the cooker, and set aside.

Add the onion, red bell pepper, and celery to the cooker. Cook for 2 minutes, stirring occasionally. Add the garlic and cook for 1 minute, or until the onion is translucent. Add the remaining oil and the beans to the cooker and stir them around. Return the chicken and sausage to the cooker and add the stock, bay leaves, parsley, and thyme.

Close and lock the lid of the cooker.

NOTE The stew can be prepared up to 2 days in advance and refrigerated, tightly covered. Reheat it over low heat, stirring occasionally. Add stock or water if the stew needs thinning after reheating.

ELECTRIC: Set the Instant Pot to cook at high pressure for 8 minutes. After 8 minutes, unplug the pot so it does not go into warming mode. Allow the pressure to return to normal naturally for 15 minutes. Quick release any remaining pressure. Remove the lid, tilting it away from you, to allow steam to escape.

OR

STOVETOP: Place the cooker over high heat and bring it to high pressure. Once high pressure is reached, reduce the heat as much as possible while still retaining the high pressure level. Cook for 6 minutes. Take the pot off the heat and allow it to return to normal pressure naturally for 15 minutes. Quick release any remaining pressure. Remove the lid, tilting it away from you, to allow steam to escape.

Remove the chicken from the cooker and cut it into bite-sized pieces. Return it to the cooker and stir it into the beans. Remove and discard the bay leaves, season with salt and hot red pepper sauce, and serve immediately.

Spicy Chicken and Rice

There's a lot going on in this very simple dish, with lots of colorful vegetables,
salty olives, and succulent dried currants as flavoring for the chicken and rice.
Serve it with a tossed salad or bowl of crunchy coleslaw on the side.

SERVES **4 to 6**

SIZE **6-quart or larger pressure cooker**

TIME **14 to 16 minutes at high pressure with quick pressure release**

When cooking rice in a pressure cooker it's important to add it to the cooker before adding the liquid. This gives the individual grains time to get coated with a bit of grease so that they don't stick to the bottom of the cooker and scorch; it also keeps the rice from getting gummy.

4 to 6 bone-in, skin-on chicken pieces of your choice (breasts cut in half, thighs, legs)
Salt and freshly ground black pepper, to taste
3 tablespoons olive oil
1 large onion, diced
1 large red bell pepper, seeds and ribs removed, diced
1 carrot, diced
1 jalapeño or serrano chile, seeds and ribs removed, finely chopped

3 garlic cloves, minced
½ cup dried currants
½ cup pitted and chopped brine-cured green olives
1½ cups long-grain white rice
2 cups Chicken Stock (page 30) or store-bought stock
4 bay leaves
¼ cup chopped fresh parsley, for serving

Pat the chicken pieces dry with paper towels and sprinkle them with salt and pepper. Heat the oil in the Instant Pot using the browning function or over medium-high heat in a stovetop cooker. Brown the chicken pieces well on all sides, turning them with tongs. Remove the chicken from the cooker and set aside.

Add the onion, red bell pepper, carrot, and chile to the cooker. Cook, stirring frequently, for 2 minutes. Add the garlic and cook for 1 minute, or until the onion is translucent. Stir in the dried currants, olives, and rice and stir well to coat the grains. Then add the stock and bay leaves. Stir well and return the chicken to the cooker.

Close and lock the lid of the cooker.

ELECTRIC: Set the Instant Pot to cook at high pressure for 16 minutes. After 16 minutes, unplug it so it does not go into warming mode. Quick release the pressure according to the manufacturer's instructions. Remove the lid, tilting it away from you, to allow steam to escape. Remove the chicken from the cooker, place it on a platter, and loosely cover it with foil. Replace the lid and allow the rice to rest for 5 minutes. Fluff the rice with a fork.

OR

STOVETOP: Place the cooker over high heat and bring it to high pressure. Once high pressure is reached, reduce the heat as much as possible while still retaining the high pressure level. Cook for 14 minutes. Take the pot off the heat and quick release the pressure according to the manufacturer's instructions. Remove the lid, tilting it away from you, to allow steam to escape. Remove the chicken from the cooker, place it on a platter, and loosely cover it with foil. Replace the lid and allow the rice to rest for 5 minutes. Fluff the rice with a fork

NOTE The dish can be prepared up to 2 days in advance and refrigerated, tightly covered. Reheat it in a 350°F oven, covered, for 20 to 25 minutes, or until hot.

VARIATION

∗ Omit the dried currants and olives from the dish and **substitute ¼ pound Spanish chorizo**, thinly sliced.

Remove and discard the bay leaves. Plate the rice next to the chicken, sprinkle each serving with parsley, and serve immediately.

Chipotle Pork and Sweet Potato Stew

Here's a hearty pork stew dominated by spicy chipotle chiles, which are smoked jalapeño chiles. Serve this dish as a stew or transfer the pork to a cutting board, shred the meat with two forks, and use it as a filling for tacos or sandwiches. You can serve the vegetables on the side.

SERVES **4 to 6**

SIZE **6-quart or larger pressure cooker**

TIME **12 to 14 minutes at high pressure with natural pressure release**

A can of chipotle chiles in adobo sauce goes a long way. Chances are you use less than a half-dozen chiles in a given recipe. To save the remainder of the can, place a few chiles with a teaspoon of sauce in ice cube trays. When they're frozen, transfer them to a heavy resealable plastic bag. Be sure to wash the ice cube tray very well before filling it with water.

1½ **pounds boneless country pork ribs**
Salt and freshly ground black pepper, to taste
2 **tablespoons olive oil**
1 **large onion, diced**
3 **garlic cloves, minced**
2 **tablespoons chili powder**
1 **tablespoon smoked Spanish paprika**
2 **teaspoons ground cumin**
1 **teaspoon dried oregano, preferably Mexican**
1 **cup lager beer**
½ **cup Chicken Stock (page 30) or store-bought stock**
2 **chipotle chiles in adobo sauce, finely chopped**
2 **tablespoons adobo sauce**
2 **large sweet potatoes, peeled and cut into 1½-inch chunks**
3 **parsnips, thickly sliced**
1 **cup fresh peas or frozen peas**
½ **cup chopped fresh cilantro, for serving**

Cut the pork into 1½-inch cubes, sprinkle it with salt and pepper, and set aside.

Heat the oil in the Instant Pot using the browning function or over medium-high heat in a stovetop cooker. Add the onion and cook, stirring frequently, for 2 minutes, or until the onion is translucent. Stir in the garlic, chili powder, paprika, cumin, and oregano and cook for 30 seconds, stirring constantly. Stir in the beer, stock, chiles, and adobo sauce. Add the pork cubes, sweet potatoes, and parsnips.

Close and lock the lid of the cooker.

ELECTRIC: Set the Instant Pot to cook at high pressure for 14 minutes. After 14 minutes, unplug the pot so it does not go into warming mode. Allow the pressure to return to normal naturally. Remove the lid, tilting it away from you, to allow steam to escape.

OR

STOVETOP: Place the cooker over high heat and bring it to high pressure. Once high pressure is reached, reduce the heat as much as possible while still retaining the high pressure level. Cook for 12 minutes. Take the pot off the heat and allow it to return to normal pressure naturally. Remove the lid, tilting it away from you, to allow steam to escape.

NOTE The dish can be prepared up to 2 days in advance and refrigerated, tightly covered. Reheat it, covered, in a 350°F oven for 20 to 25 minutes, or until hot.

Remove the pork and vegetables from the cooker with a slotted spoon and set them aside. Remove as much grease as possible from the surface of the sauce with a soup ladle. Using the browning function of the Instant Pot, or over medium-high heat, bring the liquid back to a boil. Cook until the sauce is reduced by one-third.

Add the peas to the cooker, return the meat and vegetables to reheat, and simmer for 2 minutes. Serve immediately, sprinkling the plates with cilantro.

Brisket in
Pomegranate and Wine Sauce

Pomegranate molasses should really be called pomegranate syrup. It is merely greatly reduced pomegranate juice, which gives dishes an intense fruit flavor without making them taste sweet. When it is combined with wine in the sauce, it imbues this hearty beef dish with the essence of fall. Serve it with crusty bread and a fruity red wine like a Pinot Noir from Oregon.

SERVES **4 to 6**

SIZE **6-quart or larger pressure cooker**

TIME **30 to 35 minutes at high pressure with natural pressure release**

If you can't find pomegranate molasses, you can easily make it by reducing pure pomegranate juice by two-thirds, or until it has the consistency of a syrup.

¼ cup vegetable oil, divided

2 leeks, white and pale green parts, cut into ½-inch slices

1 large sweet onion, such as Vidalia or Bermuda, halved and cut into ½-inch slices

2 garlic cloves, minced

1 (2- to 2½-pound) flat cut beef brisket

Salt and freshly ground black pepper, to taste

All-purpose flour for dredging

1 cup dry red wine

½ cup pomegranate molasses

1 tablespoon chopped fresh rosemary

½ cup chopped dried apricots

2 carrots, cut into 2-inch chunks

4 to 6 thick toast slices, for serving

½ cup pomegranate arils, for serving (optional)

Heat 2 tablespoons of the oil in the Instant Pot using the browning function or over medium-high heat in a stovetop cooker. Add the leeks and onion and cook, stirring frequently, for 2 minutes. Add the garlic and cook for 1 minute, or until the onion is translucent. Scrape the mixture out of the cooker, and set it aside.

Cut the brisket into 4 pieces, and season with salt and pepper. Dredge the meat with flour, shaking off any excess. Heat the remaining oil and add the beef, being careful not to crowd the cooker. Brown the beef on both sides and remove it from the cooker.

Add the wine to the cooker and bring to a boil. Cook for 3 minutes, then stir in the pomegranate molasses, rosemary, and dried apricots. Bring to a boil, then add the carrots and return the onion mixture and beef to the cooker.

Close and lock the lid of the cooker.

ELECTRIC: Set the Instant Pot to cook at high pressure for 35 minutes. After 35 minutes, unplug the pot so it does not go into warming mode. Allow the pressure to return to normal naturally. Remove the lid, tilting it away from you, to allow steam to escape.

OR

STOVETOP: Place the cooker over high heat and bring it to high pressure. Once high pressure is reached, reduce the heat as much as possible while still retaining the high pressure level. Cook for 30 minutes. Take the pot off the heat and allow it to return to normal pressure naturally. Remove the lid, tilting it away from you, to allow steam to escape.

Remove as much grease as possible from the surface of the sauce with a soup ladle. Using the browning function of the Instant Pot or over medium-high heat bring the liquid back to a boil. Cook until the sauce is reduced by one-fifth.

Cut the brisket into slices against the grain, and adjust the seasoning. To serve, place the meat and vegetables on top of toast slices and sprinkle with pomegranate arils, if you like.

NOTE The brisket can be prepared up to 2 days in advance and refrigerated, tightly covered. Reheat it, covered, in a 350°F oven for 20 to 25 minutes, or until hot.

VARIATION

∗ **Substitute lamb shanks** for the brisket; the cooking time remains the same.

Short Ribs with Celery, Rosemary, and Potatoes

This is one of my favorite beef dishes because of its simplicity. The aroma of rosemary blends nicely with the celery, allowing the rich hearty flavor of the meat to emerge. There are potatoes in the dish, but I frequently serve it with some oven-roasted root vegetables to add color to the plate.

SERVES **4 to 6**

SIZE **6-quart or larger pressure cooker**

TIME **30 to 35 minutes at high pressure with natural pressure release**

Short ribs are cut in two ways, and most recipes assume you're buying the English cut. These are thick pieces of beef that are cut parallel to the bones and look like rectangles. The other way, called flanken cut, are thin strips cut across the bones so many segments of bone are visible. Kalbi (or galbi) is a favorite Korean dish made with the flanken cut, and strips of flanken are also included in Eastern European soups such as borscht.

- 4 **pounds English cut short ribs, excess fat trimmed off (see note)**
- **Salt and freshly ground black pepper, to taste**
- 2 **tablespoons olive oil**
- 2 **large onions, diced large**
- 6 **celery ribs, cut into 1-inch pieces**
- 2 **garlic cloves, minced**
- 2 **cups Beef Stock (page 29) or store-bought stock**
- 3 **tablespoons chopped fresh rosemary**
- 4 to 6 **large Yukon Gold potatoes, scrubbed and left whole**
- 3 **tablespoons chopped fresh parsley, for serving**

Preheat the oven broiler and line a broiler pan with heavy-duty aluminum foil. Sprinkle the short ribs with salt and pepper, and broil them for 3 minutes per side, or until browned.

Heat the oil in the Instant Pot using the browning function or over medium-high heat in a stovetop cooker. Add the onion and celery and cook, stirring frequently, for 3 minutes, or until the onion is translucent. Stir in the garlic and cook for 30 seconds, stirring constantly. Add the stock and rosemary to the cooker, and stir well. Place the short ribs in the cooker with the meaty side down, and arrange the potatoes on top of them.

Close and lock the lid of the cooker.

ELECTRIC: Set the Instant Pot to cook at high pressure for 35 minutes. After 35 minutes, unplug the pot so it does not go into warming mode. Allow the pressure to return to normal naturally. Remove the lid, tilting it away from you, to allow steam to escape.

OR

STOVETOP: Place the cooker over high heat and bring it to high pressure. Once high pressure is reached, reduce the heat as much as possible while still retaining the high pressure level. Cook for 30 minutes. Take the pot off the heat and allow it to return to normal pressure naturally. Remove the lid, tilting it away from you, to allow steam to escape.

NOTE The short ribs can be prepared up to 2 days in advance and refrigerated, tightly covered. Reheat them, covered, in a 350°F oven for 20 to 25 minutes, or until hot.

VARIATION

∗ **Substitute** (½- to ⅔-pound) **lamb shanks** for the short ribs. The cooking time remains the same.

Remove the potatoes and short ribs from the cooker and set them aside. Remove as much grease as possible from the surface of the sauce with a soup ladle. Using the browning function of the Instant Pot or over medium-high heat bring the liquid back to a boil. Cook until the sauce is reduced by one-third.

Cut the potatoes into large chunks and return them to the cooker along with the short ribs to reheat. Season with salt and pepper, and serve, sprinkling each serving with parsley.

Lobster Risotto
with Tarragon and Fennel

Aromatic anise pairs beautifully with the sweetness of lobster, which is why tarragon is so often included as an ingredient in lobster bisque. In this risotto, anise is used in two forms, fresh fennel and tarragon. Serve the risotto with a tossed salad.

SERVES **4 to 6**

SIZE **4-quart or larger pressure cooker**

TIME **7 to 8 minutes at high pressure with quick pressure release**

Arborio isn't the only rice that can be used to make risotto. Baldo, Carnaroli, and Vialone Nano are other species that can be used. In recent years, a domestic rice marketed as Calriso—a hybrid of Italian and California species—has been added to the list. All of these species have one thing in common: a plump, short- to medium-grain size. A high content of amylopectin, a type of sticky starch, gives risotto its creamy texture.

3 tablespoons unsalted butter
2 leeks, white and pale green parts, sliced and rinsed well
½ small fennel bulb, diced
2 garlic cloves, minced
1½ cups Arborio rice
½ cup dry white wine
4 cups Seafood Stock (page 32) or store-bought stock, divided
2 tablespoons chopped fresh tarragon

2 (1¼- to 1½-pound) lobsters, cooked
½ cup fresh peas or frozen peas
Salt and freshly ground black pepper, to taste
½ cup freshly grated Parmesan cheese, for serving
Fresh fennel fronds for garnish (optional)

Melt the butter in the Instant Pot using the browning function or over medium heat in a stovetop cooker. Add the leeks and fennel, and cook, stirring occasionally, for 2 minutes. Add the garlic and cook for 1 minute, or until the leeks are translucent. Stir in the rice and cook, stirring constantly, for 2 minutes. Stir in the wine and cook for 1 minute, or until the wine is almost evaporated. Stir in 3½ cups of the stock and the tarragon.

Close and lock the lid of the cooker.

(continued on the following page)

(continued from the previous page)

ELECTRIC: Set the Instant Pot to cook at high pressure for 8 minutes. After 8 minutes, unplug the pot so it does not go into warming mode. Quick release the pressure according to the method provided by the manufacturer. Remove the lid, tilting it away from you, to allow steam to escape.

OR

STOVETOP: Place the cooker over high heat and bring it to high pressure. Once high pressure is reached, reduce the heat as much as possible while still retaining the high pressure level. Cook for 7 minutes. Quick release the pressure according to the method provided by the manufacturer. Remove the lid, tilting it away from you, to allow steam to escape.

> **NOTE** Risotto should be cooked just prior to serving.

While the rice cooks, cut the lobster meat into ¾-inch cubes. Once the pressure is released, continue to cook the risotto using the browning function of the Instant Pot or over medium heat for 3 minutes, stirring constantly, or until the liquid has thickened. Stir in the lobster meat and peas, and cook for an additional 2 minutes. Add some of the remaining stock, if needed, to achieve the proper creamy consistency. Season with salt and pepper, garnish with fennel fronds, and serve immediately. Pass around the cheese separately.

Spanish Lamb Shanks

*A bit of citrus and smoked paprika contrasted with woodsy dried mushrooms,
fresh herbs, and caramelized onions are perfect foils to the red wine braising base.
Serve the lamb with some crunchy, rustic bread and a tossed salad.*

SERVES **4 to 6**

SIZE **6-quart or larger pressure cooker**

TIME **30 to 35 minutes at high pressure with natural pressure release**

Lamb shanks range in size from ½ pound to almost 2 pounds. The size specified for this recipe will fit into a 6-quart cooker; however, if the shanks are larger, use an 8-quart cooker. The ¾-pound size are intended to be served individually, but if you're cooking larger lamb shanks, you can cut the meat off the bones once the shanks are cooked and divide the meat among the number of diners.

4 to 6 (12- to 14-ounce) lamb shanks
Salt and freshly ground black pepper, to taste
3 tablespoons olive oil
1 large sweet onion, diced
1 teaspoon granulated sugar
3 garlic cloves, minced
1 tablespoon smoked Spanish paprika
½ cup dried porcini mushrooms

2 cups Beef Stock (page 29) or store-bought stock, divided
2 oranges, washed
1½ cups dry red wine
3 tablespoons tomato paste
3 tablespoons chopped fresh rosemary
2 tablespoons chopped fresh parsley
2 bay leaves

Preheat the oven broiler and line a broiler pan with heavy-duty aluminum foil. Sprinkle the lamb with salt and pepper and broil the lamb for 3 minutes per side, or until browned.

Heat the oil in the Instant Pot using the browning function or over medium-high heat in a stovetop cooker. Add the onion and sugar, and cook, stirring frequently, for 2 minutes. Add the garlic and cook for 1 minute, or until the onion is translucent. Stir in the paprika and cook for 30 seconds, stirring constantly.

While the onion cooks, combine the mushrooms and 1 cup of the stock in a microwave-safe bowl. Microwave on high (100 percent) for 1½ minutes. Allow the mushrooms to rehydrate for 10 minutes. Remove the mushrooms from the stock with a slotted spoon, and chop them. Strain the stock through a sieve lined with a paper coffee filter or paper towel. Add the mushrooms and strained stock along with the remaining stock to the pressure cooker, and stir well.

(continued on the following page)

(continued from the previous page)

Grate the zest from oranges, and squeeze the juice from the oranges. Add the zest and orange juice to the cooker along with the wine, tomato paste, rosemary, parsley, and bay leaves. Stir well. Arrange the lamb shanks in the cooker.

Close and lock the lid of the cooker.

ELECTRIC: Set the Instant Pot to cook at high pressure for 35 minutes. After 35 minutes, unplug the pot so it does not go into warming mode. Allow the pressure to return to normal naturally. Remove the lid, tilting it away from you, to allow steam to escape.

OR

STOVETOP: Place the cooker over high heat and bring it to high pressure. Once high pressure is reached, reduce the heat as much as possible while still retaining the high pressure level. Cook for 30 minutes. Take the pot off the heat and allow it to return to normal pressure naturally. Remove the lid, tilting it away from you, to allow steam to escape.

Remove the shanks from the cooker and set them aside. Remove as much grease as possible from the surface of the sauce with a soup ladle. Remove and discard the bay leaves. Using the browning function of the Instant Pot, or over medium-high heat, bring the liquid back to a boil. Cook until the sauce is reduced by half.

Return the shanks to the sauce to reheat, season with salt and pepper, and serve.

NOTE The shanks can be prepared up to 2 days in advance and refrigerated, tightly covered. Reheat them, covered, in a 350°F oven for 20 to 25 minutes, or until hot.

Stocks

Cooking with commercial stocks—many of which are loaded with sodium—is convenient, but starting dishes with homemade stocks immediately elevates them to a higher level.

Recipes for stocks could be placed in more than one chapter in this book. I've made them in a slow cooker and allowed them to simmer away for hours in a Dutch oven. But I firmly believe that stocks are best when cooked in a pressure cooker.

The depth of flavor and body achieved in stocks with a pressure cooker is what made me an aficionado. It wasn't just the time element that convinced me that pressure cooking stocks in 1 hour, instead of 5 hours—the usual amount of time it takes to simmer stocks conventionally—was the best method. Stocks that are pressure-cooked simply taste better.

The intense heat promotes the extraction of flavor from the ingredients, both the proteins and the vegetables. And what creates the body in meat stocks is the conversion of collagen to gelatin, which the pressure cooker achieves in record time. At first I was concerned that stocks would be cloudy, because they couldn't be skimmed, but the pressure cooker prevents the liquid from bubbling so the stocks are perfectly clear.

Stocks are a great way to make use of food destined for the compost bin. Instead, reserve onion and carrot peels, the bottoms of celery ribs, and the stems from which you've stripped the leaves of fresh parsley, and keep them in a bag in the freezer to use later for making stock.

If you take the time to bone your own chicken breasts or cut up your own beef stew meat from a roast, then you have everything you need to make stock. I make stock on a weekly basis, so most often I buy all the necessary ingredients, as well as take advantage of scraps.

I do not add salt to any to the stocks, which gives you much more versatility when using them. While you may choose to add salt to a stock that you want to use for making soup, there may also be times when you want to drastically reduce a stock to form a sauce. Reducing a salted stock will give you an inedible result, because the salinity rises as the water evaporates during reduction.

There is one negative aspect to making stocks in the pressure cooker, however. I really miss the aroma that used to fill the house when a stockpot simmered all day on the stove.

Beef Stock

While beef stock is not called for as often as chicken stock in recipes, it is the backbone of certain dishes. Beef shank is about the least expensive cut of beef that makes good stock, but I urge you to get a chuck roast, cut off the meat to make beef stew, and then use the bones to make stock.

MAKES **3 quarts**

SIZE **6-quart or larger pressure cooker**

TIME **80 to 90 minutes at high pressure with natural pressure release**

Most really good restaurants make veal stock instead of beef stock, but they have access to veal bones that we would have to spend a fortune for, since the least expensive cut of veal is the shank cooked for osso buco. Another option is breast of veal, which is difficult to find, too.

NOTE The stock can be refrigerated and used within 3 days, or it can be frozen for up to 6 months.

VARIATION

∗ **Beef Bone Broth**: Add 3 tablespoons of cider vinegar to the cooker and cook the broth for 4½ hours in an electric cooker and 4 hours in a stovetop cooker.

2 **pounds beef trimmings (bones, fat) or inexpensive beef shank**
1 **celery rib, sliced**
1 **medium onion, sliced**
1 **carrot, trimmed, scrubbed, and cut into thick slices**
1 **tablespoon whole black peppercorns**
4 **garlic cloves, peeled**
3 **sprigs fresh parsley**
2 **sprigs fresh thyme**
2 **bay leaves**

Preheat the oven broiler, and line a broiler pan with heavy-duty aluminum foil. Broil the beef bones for 3 minutes per side, or until browned. Transfer the beef to the pressure cooker, and add 3 quarts of water, the celery, onion, carrot, peppercorns, garlic, parsley, thyme, and bay leaves. Close and lock the lid of the cooker.

ELECTRIC: Set the Instant Pot to cook at high pressure for 90 minutes. After 90 minutes, unplug the pot so it does not go into warming mode. Allow the pressure to return to normal naturally. Remove the lid, tilting it away from you, to allow steam to escape.

OR

STOVETOP: Place the cooker over high heat and bring it to high pressure. Once high pressure is reached, reduce the heat as much as possible while still retaining the high pressure level. Cook for 80 minutes. Take the pot off the heat and allow it to return to normal pressure naturally. Remove the lid, tilting it away from you, to allow steam to escape.

Strain the stock through a fine-meshed sieve, pushing with the back of a spoon to extract as much liquid as possible. Discard the solids, and spoon the stock into smaller containers. Refrigerate once the stock reaches room temperature. Then remove and discard the layer of fat from the surface of the stock.

Chicken Stock

This is the most important stock, because it's used for pork and veal dishes as well as soups and, of course, poultry dishes. The good thing about making this stock is you actually get more flavor from the inexpensive parts of the bird, like the leg quarters and backs.

MAKES **3 quarts**

SIZE **6-quart or larger pressure cooker**

TIME **80 to 90 minutes at high pressure with natural pressure release**

The giblets—the neck, heart, and gizzard—are in the little bag you find inside a whole chicken, which you probably usually throw away. Save them all for stock, but freeze the chicken liver separately. Livers cannot be used in stock, but once you have enough of them, you can make a pâté, or sauté the livers for dinner. If you live near an Asian market you might also be able to buy chicken feet. They make wonderful stock.

NOTE The stock can be refrigerated and used within 3 days, or it can be frozen for up to 6 months.

3 **pounds chicken pieces (backs, giblets, leg quarters, wings)**
2 **tablespoons vegetable oil**
3 **celery ribs, cut into thick slices**
2 **onions, quartered**
2 **carrots, cut into thick slices**
2 **tablespoons whole black peppercorns**
6 **garlic cloves, peeled**
4 **sprigs fresh parsley**
3 **sprigs fresh thyme**
2 **bay leaves**

Hack the chicken into 2-inch pieces with a sharp knife or cleaver.

Heat the oil in the Instant Pot using the browning function or over medium-high heat in a stovetop cooker. Add some of the chicken parts, skin side down, and brown them well. Add 3 quarts of water to the cooker along with the celery, onions, carrots, peppercorns, garlic, parsley, thyme, and bay leaves.

Close and lock the lid of the cooker.

ELECTRIC: Set the Instant Pot to cook at high pressure for 90 minutes. After 90 minutes, unplug the pot so it does not go into warming mode. Allow the pressure to return to normal naturally. Remove the lid, tilting it away from you, to allow steam to escape.

OR

STOVETOP: Place the cooker over high heat and bring it to high pressure. Once high pressure is reached, reduce the heat as much as possible while still retaining the high pressure level. Cook for 80 minutes. Take the pot off the heat and allow it to return to normal pressure naturally. Remove the lid, tilting it away from you, to allow steam to escape.

Strain the stock through a fine-meshed sieve, pushing with the back of a spoon to extract as much liquid as possible. Discard the solids, spoon the stock into smaller containers, and refrigerate when the stock reaches room temperature. Remove and discard the fat layer from the surface of the stock once chilled.

VARIATIONS

∗ **Turkey Stock**: Substitute 3 pounds of turkey giblets for the chicken pieces and add 2 sprigs of fresh sage to the cooker.

∗ **Chicken Bone Broth**: Add 3 tablespoons of cider vinegar to the cooker and cook the broth for 3 hours in an electric cooker and 2½ hours in a stovetop cooker.

∗ **Chinese Chicken Stock**: Substitute 2 bunches of scallions for the onions, substitute cilantro for the parsley and thyme, omit the carrots and bay leaves, and add ½ cup thickly sliced fresh ginger to the cooker.

∗ **Ham Stock**: Substitute 3 pounds of smoked ham hocks for the chicken parts (there is no need to brown them).

Seafood Stock

Seafood stock is a key to the rich flavor of fish and seafood soups and stews, so make friends with the staff of your local fish store or the seafood counter of your supermarket. They frequently have skeletons or fish heads around from creating fillets and will often give you some gratis.

MAKES **3 quarts**

SIZE **6-quart or larger pressure cooker**

TIME **60 to 70 minutes at high pressure with natural pressure release**

Seafood stock is perhaps the least convenient to make, if you don't live near the coast or go to a supermarket with a good seafood department. Seafood stock can now be bought in most stores, however, and another good substitute is bottled clam juice. Use it in place of the water, and simmer it with vegetables and wine to intensify its flavor.

NOTE The stock can be refrigerated and used within 3 days, or it can be frozen for up to 6 months.

VARIATION

＊**Lobster Stock**: Substitute the shells, small swimmeret legs, and internal skeletons of 3 or 4 (1½-pound) lobsters, broken up into small pieces, for the fish skin and bones.

2 **pounds bones and skin from firm-fleshed white fish such as halibut, cod, or sole**
Shells from **3 pounds raw shrimp (optional)**
1 **cup dry white wine**
2 **(3-inch) pieces lemon zest**
1 **carrot, trimmed and cut into 1-inch chunks**
1 **medium onion, peeled and sliced**
1 **celery rib, sliced**
1 **tablespoon whole black peppercorns**
3 **sprigs fresh parsley**
2 **sprigs fresh thyme**
2 **sprigs fresh tarragon**
2 **garlic cloves, peeled**
1 **bay leaf**

Place the fish trimmings in the cooker and add the shrimp shells, if using. Add 3 quarts of water, along with the wine, lemon zest, carrot, onion, celery, peppercorns, parsley, thyme, tarragon, garlic, and bay leaf.

Close and lock the lid of the cooker.

ELECTRIC: Set the Instant Pot to cook at high pressure for 70 minutes. After 70 minutes, unplug the pot so it does not go into warming mode. Allow the pressure to return to normal naturally. Remove the lid, tilting it away from you, to allow steam to escape.

OR

STOVETOP: Place the cooker over high heat and bring it to high pressure. Once high pressure is reached, reduce the heat as much as possible while still retaining the high pressure level. Cook for 1 hour. Take the pot off the heat and allow it to return to normal pressure naturally. Remove the lid, tilting it away from you, to allow steam to escape.

Strain the stock through a fine-meshed sieve, pushing with the back of a spoon to extract as much liquid as possible. Discard the solids and spoon the stock into smaller containers. Refrigerate the stock once it reaches room temperature.

Vegetable Stock

You may not think it's necessary to use vegetable stock if you're making a vegetarian dish that includes the same vegetables, but that's not the case. Using vegetable stock creates a much more richly flavored soup that can't be replicated by simply increasing the quantity of vegetables in the soup recipe.

MAKES **3 quarts**

SIZE **6-quart or larger pressure cooker**

TIME **60 to 70 minutes at high pressure with natural pressure release**

While it's fine to save carrot peels and parsley stems to use in stocks, discard the dark green tops of leeks because they make stocks taste bitter and somewhat grassy. They're good for composting, however.

NOTE The stock can be refrigerated and used within 3 days, or it can be frozen for up to 6 months.

2 **carrots, scrubbed, trimmed, and thinly sliced**
2 **celery ribs, sliced**
2 **leeks, white part and pale green parts only, thinly sliced and rinsed well**
1 **small onion, peeled and thinly sliced**
1 **tablespoon whole black peppercorns**
4 **sprigs fresh parsley**
3 **sprigs fresh thyme**
2 **sprigs fresh rosemary**
2 **garlic cloves, peeled**
1 **bay leaf**

Pour 3 quarts of water into the cooker and add the carrots, celery, leeks, onion, peppercorns, parsley, thyme, rosemary, garlic, and bay leaf.

Close and lock the lid of the cooker.

ELECTRIC: Set the Instant Pot to cook at high pressure for 70 minutes. After 70 minutes, unplug the pot so it does not go into warming mode. Allow the pressure to return to normal naturally. Remove the lid, tilting it away from you, to allow steam to escape.

OR

STOVETOP: Place the cooker over high heat and bring it to high pressure. Once high pressure is reached, reduce the heat as much as possible while still retaining the high pressure level. Cook for 1 hour. Take the pot off the heat and allow it to return to normal pressure naturally. Remove the lid, tilting it away from you, to allow steam to escape.

Strain the stock through a fine-meshed sieve, pushing with the back of a spoon to extract as much liquid as possible. Discard the solids, and spoon the stock into smaller containers. Refrigerate once the stock reaches room temperature.

chapter 2

Slow Cookers

It sounds like a paradox to say that using a slow cooker is totally consistent with our fast-paced world, but it's a fact. Slow cookers give us the flexibility to be away from home for hours at a time without fear of ruined food or—perish the thought—a fire.

And what greets you, after being away for hours, is instant gratification; your slow cooker has produced a delicious, healthful dish that is better for your body *and* your budget than nutritionally bankrupt fast food.

Rival introduced the first slow cooker, the Crock-Pot, in 1971, and the introductory slogan remains true more than 45 years later: it "cooks all day while the cook's away." Like such trademarked brand names as Kleenex® for paper facial tissue or Formica® for plastic laminate, Crock-Pot has almost become synonymous with the slow cooker. However, not every slow cooker is a Crock-Pot, so the generic term is used in this book.

Slow cookers use indirect heat to cook food at a low temperature for an extended period of time. Direct heat is the power of a stove burner underneath a pot; indirect heat is the overall heat that surrounds food in the oven. Think of it this way: if you're standing on a hot sidewalk, you're feeling direct heat on the soles of your feet, but the heat you feel all over your body when you're lounging on the beach under the sun is warm, indirect heat.

Anatomy of a Slow Cooker

Slow cookers come in both round and oval shapes, and the one you select depends on how you plan to use it most often. I find that oval slow cookers are better for large roasts, as they hold the shape of most pot roasts. However, round slow cookers are preferable for stews and beans dishes because they surround the food at an equal distance rather than having hotter or colder zones.

Regardless of shape, the operation of all slow cookers remains almost the same. While some newer models with browning functions have a metal insert, almost all older slow cookers use pottery that fits inside a metal housing and are topped with a clear glass or plastic lid. Removing the lid while food is cooking is not a good idea because it lengthens the time needed to cook the dish, so manufacturers make them clear (you can easily clear any steam or condensation that collect on the lid by jiggling it). The now-popular Instant Pot can also serve as a slow cooker, and you can purchase an inexpensive Instant Pot ceramic inner pot, as well as a clear lid, to use the appliance as a slow cooker.

Wrap-around heating elements encased between the slow cooker's outer and inner layers of metal cook the food. The coils never directly touch the crockery insert. As the element heats, it gently warms the air between the two layers of metal, and it is the hot air that touches the crockery. This construction eliminates the need for stirring ingredients in order to distribute heat, because no part of the pot gets hotter than any other.

The largest variation in slow cookers is size, which ranges from tiny 1-quart models that are excellent for hot dips and fondue, to gigantic 7-quart models that are fairly useless, unless you are cooking very large batches of food for a large family, in which case they are excellent choices.

SLOW COOKER HINTS AND CAUTIONS

Cooking in a slow cooker does not require any culinary techniques beyond the basics that you've used for years. You're slicing and dicing food, sometimes browning it, and measuring other ingredients accurately. But slow cookers can be perplexing if you're not accustomed to using one. Here are some general tips to help you master slow cooker conundrums:

* Remember that cooking times are wide approximations *within hours* rather than minutes! That's because the age or power of a slow cooker, and the temperature of ingredients, must be taken into account. Check the food at the beginning of the stated range, and then gauge if it needs more time, and about how much time. If you're cooking on low and the carrots or cubes of potato are still rock-hard, for example, turn the heat to high and realize that you're looking at another hour or so.

* Foods cook faster on the bottom of a slow cooker than at the top because there are heat coils on the bottom of the pan but not at the top, which merely has a cover.

* Don't add dairy products except at the end of the cooking time, as noted in the recipes. They can curdle if they are cooked too long.

* Season dishes with pepper at the end of cooking, because the flavor can become harsh after cooking for a long time.

* You can trim hours off a slow-cooked meal by using boiling rather than chilled or room-temperature liquid. To test how much time can be trimmed, place the amount of liquid in the slow cooker and see how long it takes to come to a boil on high. Don't subtract that time from the total cooking time, because the temperature of the other ingredients will vary, so subtract half the time.

* Do not preheat the empty insert while you're preparing the food because it could crack when you add cold food.

* Never submerge the metal casing in water or fill it with water. While the inside of the metal does occasionally get dirty, it's best to clean it with an abrasive cleaner and then give it a wipe with a damp cloth or paper towel. While a less than pristine metal casing may not be aesthetically pleasing, do remember that food never touches the metal, so if there are a few drips here and there it's not really important.

(continued on the following page)

* Resist the temptation to stir. Every time you take the lid off the slow cooker you'll need to compensate for heat loss by adding 10 minutes to the cooking time if the temperature is on high, and 20 minutes if the temperature is on low. Certain recipes in this chapter, however, especially those for fish, instruct you to add ingredients during the cooking time. In those cases, the heat loss from opening the pot has been factored into the total cooking time.

* Always fill a slow cooker between one-half and two-thirds full, so that it will cook properly, as well as for food safety: a slow cooker should always be at least half full so it can generate the necessary steam to kill bacteria. On the other hand, you don't want a slow cooker to be more than two-thirds full or the food in the center will not pass through the "danger zone" for bacterial growth of 40°F to 145°F quickly enough.

* Don't add more liquid to a slow cooker recipe than is specified in the recipe. Even if the food is not submerged in liquid when you start, foods such as meats and vegetables give off liquid as they cook; in the slow cooker that additional liquid does not evaporate.

With few exceptions—such as a few meat dishes—all recipes in this book were written for and tested in a 4- or 5-quart slow cooker; that is what is meant by medium. Either a 4- or 5-quart slow cooker makes enough for four to eight people, depending on the recipe.

Moroccan Garbanzo Bean and Vegetable Stew

Most cuisines around the Mediterranean feature garbanzo beans. In the Middle East, Italy, and North Africa they're used extensively in soups and stews. This stew has a vivid color to match its flavor.

SERVES **4 to 6**

SIZE **Medium slow cooker (4 or 5 quarts)**

TIME **Minimum of 3½ hours**

Turmeric is the root of a tropical plant, and it's what gives American mustard its distinctive yellow color. Turmeric is sometimes called "poor man's saffron" because it gives food a similar bright yellow hue, but it doesn't have the same fragrance as saffron and has a stronger flavor.

NOTE The dish can be prepared up to 2 days in advance and refrigerated, tightly covered. Reheat it, covered, over low heat until hot, stirring occasionally.

VARIATION

* **Substitute lima beans** for the garbanzo beans, and substitute 2 tablespoons Italian seasoning for the cumin, coriander, turmeric, and cinnamon.

2 cups dried garbanzo beans
3 tablespoons olive oil
2 large onions, diced
3 garlic cloves, minced
1 tablespoon ground cumin
2 teaspoons ground coriander
1 teaspoon ground turmeric
¼ teaspoon ground cinnamon
1 (28-ounce) can diced tomatoes, drained
4 cups Vegetable Stock (page 33) or store-bought stock
⅓ pound carrots, thickly sliced
¼ pound parsnips, thickly sliced
Salt and freshly ground black pepper, to taste

Rinse the beans in a colander and place them in a mixing bowl covered with cold salted water. Allow the beans to soak for a minimum of 6 hours or overnight. Or place the beans in a saucepan of salted water and bring to a boil over high heat. Boil 1 minute. Turn off the heat, cover the pan, and soak the beans for 1 hour. Drain the beans, discard the soaking water, rinse them well, and cook or refrigerate the beans as soon as possible.

Heat the oil using the browning function of the cooker or in a medium skillet over medium-high heat. Add the onions and cook them, stirring frequently, for 2 minutes. Add the garlic and cook for 1 minute, or until the onions are translucent. Turn off the browning function or reduce the heat to low if using a skillet. Stir in the cumin, coriander, turmeric, and cinnamon. Cook for 1 minute, stirring constantly. Scrape the mixture into the slow cooker if using a skillet.

Place the drained beans in the slow cooker. Add the tomatoes, stock, carrots, and parsnips, and stir well. Cook on low for 7 to 8 hours or on high for 3½ to 4 hours, or until the garbanzo beans are tender. Season with salt and pepper during the last hour of cooking time.

White Bean and Tuna Salad

A slow cooker adds so little heat to the kitchen that it's a boon for summer cooking, when the thought of lighting even a stovetop burner is not appealing. And bean salads are a year-round treat, especially one like this, which is enlivened with herbs in a tasty citrus dressing.

SERVES **4 to 6**

SIZE **Medium slow cooker (4 or 5 quarts)**

TIME **Minimum of 2 hours**   CHILLING TIME **Minimum of 2 hours**

Until the 1980s almost all tuna was packed in some sort of edible oil, and back then cans weighed 6.5 ounces. The vast majority of tuna found in American markets today is packed in water. Personally, I don't think water-packed tuna delivers the same texture and flavor as oil-packed, even after mayonnaise has been added, and I never use it. And one of the nutritional advantages of tuna packed in oil is the omega-3 fatty acids in the tuna that find their way into the oil. Using the oil the tuna is packed in gives you all of its nutritional benefits.

NOTE The dish can be made up to 1 day in advance and refrigerated, tightly covered.

VARIATION

* **Substitute ½ pound diced cooked shrimp** for the tuna fish and increase the amount of olive oil in the dressing to ½ cup.

1 **pound dried white navy beans**
3 **garlic cloves, minced**
2 **bay leaves**
3 **(5-ounce) cans tuna packed in olive oil, drained with the oil reserved**
⅓ **cup finely chopped fresh parsley**
4 **scallions, white parts and 4 inches of green tops, chopped**
⅓ **cup freshly squeezed lemon juice**
¼ **cup olive oil**
Salt and freshly ground black pepper, to taste
⅓ **cup olive oil**

Rinse the beans in a colander and place them in a mixing bowl covered with cold salted water. Allow the beans to soak for a minimum of 6 hours or overnight. Or place the beans into a saucepan of salted water and bring to a boil over high heat. Boil 1 minute. Turn off the heat, cover the pan, and soak the beans for 1 hour. Drain the beans, discard the soaking water, rinse them well, and cook or refrigerate the beans as soon as possible.

Transfer the beans to the slow cooker, pour in enough water to cover the beans by 2 inches, and add the garlic and bay leaves. Cook on low for 4 to 6 hours or on high for 2 to 3 hours or until the beans are tender. Add salt prior to the last hour of cooking time. Drain the beans, remove and discard the bay leaves, and chill them well. Break the tuna into bite-sized pieces and add it to the beans.

Combine the parsley and scallions in a mixing bowl, and stir in the lemon juice. Mix well, add the oil from the tuna cans, the additional olive oil, and mix well again. Gently stir the dressing into the beans, season with salt and pepper, and serve chilled.

Italian Lamb Stew

Cipollini onions look like tiny hockey pucks when you see them in the market, and they hold their shape very well when braised, which makes them perfect for the slow cooker. This stew is a complete one-dish meal, since it also contains potatoes and carrots.

SERVES **4 to 6**

SIZE **Large slow cooker (7 quarts)**

TIME **Minimum of 4 hours**

If a potato has a greenish tinge, it means that it's been exposed to light. Cut away that portion of the potato because the green flesh can be toxic. Store potatoes in a cool, dry place—but not with onions. Onions give off a natural gas that can cause potatoes to quickly spoil.

NOTE The dish can be prepared up to 2 days in advance and refrigerated, tightly covered. Reheat it, covered, in a 350°F oven for 20 to 25 minutes, or until hot.

VARIATION

∗ **Substitute cubes of beef chuck** for the lamb shoulder.

1½ pounds boneless lamb shoulder or leg of lamb, fat trimmed and cut into 2-inch cubes
All-purpose flour for dredging
¼ cup olive oil
1 small yellow onion, diced
3 garlic cloves, minced
1 pound cipollini onions, peeled
12 small redskin potatoes, scrubbed and halved
2 carrots, thickly sliced
1½ cups Beef Stock (page 29) or store-bought stock
1 cup dry red wine
1 (14.5-ounce) can diced tomatoes, undrained
2 tablespoons chopped fresh rosemary
2 tablespoons chopped fresh parsley
1 bay leaf
Salt and freshly ground black pepper, to taste

Coat the lamb with the flour, shaking off any excess. Heat the oil in the slow cooker using the browning function or in a large skillet over medium-high heat. Add the lamb cubes and brown them on all sides. Remove the lamb from the pan with a slotted spoon, and set it aside.

Add the yellow onion. Cook, stirring frequently, for 2 minutes. Add the garlic and cook for 1 minute, or until the onion is translucent. Scrape the mixture into the slow cooker, if using a skillet.

Return the lamb to the slow cooker and add the cipollini onions, potatoes, carrots, stock, wine, tomatoes, rosemary, parsley, and bay leaf, and stir well.

Cook on low for 8 to 10 hours or on high for 4 to 5 hours, or until the lamb and vegetables are tender. Remove as much grease as possible from the surface of the stew with a soup ladle. Remove and discard the bay leaf, season with salt and pepper, and serve hot.

Fish Stew with Potatoes and Kale

Every cuisine that developed near a body of water has a wonderful selection of fish stews that were created by the fishermen with whatever they caught in the nets that day. This hearty stew is topped with a dollop of a garlicky mayonnaise. Some crusty bread is a nice addition to the table.

SERVES **4 to 6**

SIZE **Medium slow cooker (4 or 5 quarts)**

TIME **Minimum of 3¾ hours**

You can use curly kale and Tuscan kale interchangeably in recipes, but the technique for prepping it is slightly different. For curly kale, just pull hunks away from the stem and central rib and you're all set. To prep the flat leaves of Tuscan kale, run a paring knife on either side of the central rib and then cut the leaves.

- 1½ **pounds halibut, cod, monkfish, snapper, sea bass, or any firm-fleshed white fish**
- 2 **tablespoons olive oil**
- 2 **medium onions, diced**
- 8 **garlic cloves, minced, divided**
- 4 **cups Seafood Stock (page 32) or store-bought stock**
- ½ **cup dry white wine**
- 2 **tablespoons freshly squeezed lemon juice**
- 1 **pound redskin potatoes, scrubbed and cut into ¾-inch dice**
- 2 **tablespoons chopped fresh parsley**
- 1 **tablespoon fresh thyme**
- 1 **bay leaf**
- ½ **pound kale**
- ½ **cup mayonnaise**
- 1 **teaspoon grated lemon zest**

Salt and freshly ground black pepper, to taste

Rinse the fish and pat it dry with paper towels. Remove and discard any skin or bones. Cut the fish into 1-inch cubes. Tightly wrap the fish with plastic wrap and refrigerate the fish until ready to use.

Heat the oil in the slow cooker using the browning function or in a small skillet over medium-high heat. Add the onion and half the garlic, and cook, stirring frequently, for 3 minutes, or until the onion is translucent. Scrape the mixture into the slow cooker if using a skillet.

Add the stock, wine, lemon juice, potatoes, parsley, thyme, and bay leaf to the slow cooker, and stir well. Cook on low for 6 to 8 hours or on high for 3 to 4 hours, or until the potatoes are tender.

While the stew cooks, prepare the kale. Rinse the leaves, and discard the stems. Cut the leaves crosswise into ½-inch slices.

Make the sauce by combining the mayonnaise, lemon zest, and remaining garlic. Refrigerate until ready to serve.

If cooking on low, raise the heat to high. Add the fish and kale. Cook for 40 to 55 minutes, or until the fish is just cooked through and flakes easily. Remove and discard the bay leaf, season with salt and pepper, and serve hot. Pass the sauce separately.

NOTE The stew can be prepared up to 3 days in advance and refrigerated, tightly covered. Reheat it, covered, over low heat, stirring occasionally.

VARIATION

∗ **Substitute Swiss chard or escarole** for the kale.

Monkfish with Cabbage, Pancetta, Potatoes, and Rosemary

Monkfish, sometimes called poor man's lobster because its sweet flavor and texture is similar to the prized crustacean and popular in a lot of Mediterranean cooking. This preparation, scented with rosemary and made somewhat hearty with pancetta, is inspired by a dish served in the Veneto.

SERVES **4 to 6**

SIZE **Medium slow cooker (4 or 5 quarts)**

TIME **Minimum of 2 hours**

> Cabbage is clearly one of the sturdier vegetables, and it will keep refrigerated for up to 6 weeks if not cut. Looser heads like Savoy and Napa cabbage should be used within 3 weeks. Do not wash cabbage before storing it because moisture will bring on decay.

- ¾ pound (½ of a small head) Savoy or green cabbage
- ¼ pound pancetta, diced
- 1½ pounds monkfish fillets, trimmed and cut into serving pieces
- 1 pound Yukon Gold potatoes, peeled and cut into 1-inch cubes
- 2 garlic cloves, minced
- 1½ cups Seafood Stock (page 32) or store-bought stock
- ½ cup dry white wine
- 2 tablespoons chopped fresh rosemary
- 1 tablespoon chopped fresh parsley
- 2 teaspoons grated lemon zest
- 2 tablespoons unsalted butter
- Salt and freshly ground black pepper, to taste

Rinse and core the cabbage. Cut it into wedges and then shred it. Set aside.

Cook the pancetta using the browning function of the slow cooker or in a heavy skillet over medium heat for 5 to 7 minutes, or until crisp. Remove the pancetta from the pan with a slotted spoon, and set it aside. Add the monkfish to the slow cooker (or place the sections in the skillet) and brown it on all sides in the fat. Refrigerate the monkfish wrapped in plastic wrap. Scrape the mixture into the slow cooker if using a skillet.

Add the cabbage, potatoes, garlic, stock, wine, rosemary, parsley, and lemon zest to the slow cooker, and stir well. Cook on low for 3 to 4 hours or on high for 1 to 1½ hours, or until the vegetables are almost tender.

If cooking on low, raise the heat to high. Season the monkfish with salt and pepper, and place it on top of the vegetables. Cook the monkfish for 30 to 45 minutes, or until it is cooked through. Remove the monkfish from the slow cooker, and keep it warm. Add the butter to the vegetables, and stir to melt the butter. Season with salt and pepper.

To serve, mound some of the vegetables onto each plate. Slice the monkfish into medallions and arrange the slices on top of the cabbage.

NOTE The vegetable mixture can be cooked up to 2 days in advance and refrigerated, tightly covered. Reheat it in a microwave oven or over low heat, and return it to the slow cooker. The fish should be cooked just prior to serving.

VARIATION

* **Substitute thick fillets of halibut or cod**; the cooking time will remain the same.

Mexican Turkey Meatball and Rice Soup

(Sopa Albondigas)

Adding cornmeal to the meatball mixture in this recipe adds a distinctive flavor and also helps to keep the meatballs together as they cook. Serve this hearty main dish soup with some warm corn tortillas.

MAKES **4 to 6 servings**

SIZE **Medium slow cooker (4 or 5 quarts)**

TIME **Minimum of 3 hours**

The easiest way to break apart a whole head of garlic is to slam the root end onto the countertop. It should then separate easily into individual cloves.

- 1½ **pounds ground turkey**
- ¼ **cup yellow cornmeal**
- ¼ **cup milk**
- 1 **large egg, lightly beaten**
- 2 **tablespoons chili powder, divided**
- **Salt and freshly ground black pepper, to taste**
- 2 **tablespoons olive oil**
- 1 **large onion, diced**
- 4 **garlic cloves, minced**
- 1 **teaspoon ground cumin**
- ½ **teaspoon dried oregano, preferably Mexican**

- 1 **(28-ounce) can diced tomatoes, undrained**
- 4 **cups Chicken Stock (page 30) or store-bought stock**
- ½ **cup refrigerated tomato salsa**
- 1 **teaspoon hot red pepper sauce, or to taste**
- 2 **tablespoons chopped fresh cilantro**
- 1 **large carrot, diced**
- 1 **celery rib, diced**
- ¾ **cup long-grain rice**
- 1 **(15-ounce) can kidney beans, drained and rinsed**

Combine the turkey, cornmeal, milk, egg, 1 tablespoon of the chili powder, salt, and pepper in a mixing bowl, and mix well. Form the mixture into 1-inch balls.

Heat the oil in the slow cooker using the browning function or in a medium skillet over medium-high heat. Add the meatballs and brown them, turning them gently with tongs. Remove the meatballs from the pan and set them aside.

Add the onion to the oil, and cook, stirring frequently, for 2 minutes. Add the garlic and cook for 1 minute or until the onion is translucent. Stir in the remaining chili powder, along with the cumin and oregano. Scrape the mixture into the slow cooker if using a skillet.

Add the tomatoes, stock, salsa, hot red pepper sauce, and cilantro to the slow cooker, and stir well. Return the meatballs to the slow cooker and add the carrot and celery.

Cook on low for 4 to 6 hours or on high for 2 to 3 hours, or until the liquid is boiling. Stir in the rice and beans and cook for an additional 2 hours on low or 1 hour on high, or until the meatballs are cooked through and the rice is tender. Season with salt and pepper, and serve hot.

NOTE The soup can be prepared up to 3 days in advance and refrigerated, tightly covered. Reheat it, covered, over low heat, stirring occasionally.

VARIATION

✳ **Substitute a combination of ground pork and ground beef** for the turkey, and **substitute beef stock** for the chicken stock.

Chicken with Potatoes and Olives

The combination of bell peppers and olives is characteristic of the cooking from much of Sicily, especially the region around Syracuse. This dish gets even more flavor from the addition of some salty capers and a bit of vinegar, and it goes well with a crunchy bread and tossed salad. It's a meal that is simultaneously light and vibrant.

SERVES **4 to 6**

SIZE **Medium slow cooker (4 or 5 quarts)**

TIME **Minimum of 3¼ hours**

In the seventeenth century, King Henry IV of France's prime minister Sully used "a chicken in every pot" as a metaphor for the prosperity he wished for his citizens. In the 1600s, chickens were associated with luxury, rather than with fast food, and they were only eaten on holidays.

- **4 to 6 bone-in, skin-on chicken pieces of your choice (breasts cut in half, thighs, legs)**
- **Salt and freshly ground black pepper, to taste**
- **¼ cup olive oil**
- **1 large red onion, halved and thinly sliced**
- **2 celery ribs, sliced**
- **1 red bell pepper, seeds and ribs removed, thinly sliced**
- **1 orange bell pepper, seeds and ribs removed, thinly sliced**
- **2 garlic cloves, minced**
- **1 pound redskin potatoes, scrubbed and cut into 1-inch cubes**
- **1 (14.5-ounce) can diced tomatoes, undrained**
- **1½ cups Chicken Stock (page 30) or store-bought stock**
- **1 tablespoon fresh thyme leaves**
- **½ cup sliced brine-cured green olives, preferably Sicilian**
- **2 tablespoons capers, drained and rinsed**
- **2 tablespoons cider vinegar**

Pat the chicken pieces dry with paper towels and sprinkle the pieces with salt and pepper.

Heat the oil in the slow cooker using the browning function or in a large skillet over medium-high heat. Add the chicken pieces, being careful not to crowd the pan. Brown the pieces well on all sides, turning them gently with tongs. Remove the chicken from the pan and set it aside.

Add the onion, celery, red bell pepper, and orange bell pepper to the oil. Cook, stirring frequently, for 2 minutes. Add the garlic and cook for 1 minute, or until the onion is translucent. Scrape the mixture into the slow cooker if using a skillet.

Return the chicken pieces to the slow cooker and add the potatoes, tomatoes, stock, thyme, olives, capers, and vinegar. Stir well. Cook on low for 6 to 8 hours or on high for 3 to 4 hours, or until the chicken is cooked through, tender, and no longer pink. Season with salt and pepper, and serve hot.

NOTE The dish can be prepared up to 2 days in advance and refrigerated, tightly covered. Reheat it, covered, in a 350°F oven for 20 to 25 minutes, or until hot.

VARIATION

* **Substitute cubes of pork loin** for the chicken; the cooking time will remain the same.

Turkey Tonnato
with Vinaigrette Vegetables

Chilled turkey with tuna sauce is a delicious combination, and the vegetables take on a vibrant flavor from being cooked with it. This is a riff on the Italian classic that naps slices of poached veal in a similar sauce.

SERVES 4 to 6

SIZE Medium slow cooker (4 or 5 quarts)

COOKING TIME Minimum of 3 hours   CHILLING TIME Minimum of 8 hours

Although there is no use for the braising liquid in this recipe, it's a richly flavored stock and it's a shame to throw it away. Freeze it and use it in place of chicken stock when cooking another recipe.

TURKEY AND VEGETABLES

½ (1½-pound) boneless, skinless turkey breast
3 garlic cloves, peeled and cut into quarters
1½ cups Chicken Stock (page 30) or store-bought stock
½ cup dry white wine
1 onion, diced
2 carrots, cut into 1-inch chunks
2 large redskin potatoes, cut into 1-inch chunks
4 sprigs fresh parsley
2 sprigs fresh thyme
1 bay leaf
Salt and freshly ground black pepper, to taste

TUNA SAUCE

2 (5-ounce) cans imported tuna packed in olive oil, undrained
¼ cup freshly squeezed lemon juice
2 tablespoons anchovy paste
¼ cup mayonnaise
2 tablespoons capers, drained and rinsed
Salt and freshly ground black pepper, to taste

VINAIGRETTE

3 tablespoons white wine vinegar
1 tablespoon grainy mustard
2 teaspoons sugar
1 teaspoon fresh thyme leaves
Salt and freshly ground black pepper, to taste
½ cup olive oil

Place the turkey breast between two sheets of plastic wrap. Pound it with the flat side of a meat mallet or bottom of a small saucepan until it is a uniform thickness. Roll the turkey breast into a shape that will fit into your slow cooker, and tie it with kitchen string. Make 12 slits around the turkey breast, and insert a garlic quarter in each one.

Place the turkey breast in the slow cooker, and add the stock, wine, onion, carrots, and potatoes. Tie the parsley, thyme, and bay leaf in cheesecloth or stuff them into a tea infuser and place them in the pot. Season with salt and pepper. Cook on low for 6 to 8 hours or on high for 3 to 4 hours, or until a thermometer inserted in the center of the turkey registers 165°F on an instant-read thermometer. Remove the turkey and vegetables from the slow cooker and chill well in separate bowls. Remove and discard the herbs.

For the tuna sauce, combine the tuna, lemon juice, and anchovy paste in a food processor fitted with a steel blade or in a blender. Puree until smooth, and scrape the mixture into a mixing bowl. Stir in the mayonnaise and capers, and season with salt and pepper.

For the vinaigrette, combine the vinegar, mustard, sugar, thyme, salt, and pepper in a jar with a tight-fitting lid. Shake well to dissolve the sugar and salt. Add the olive oil and shake well again. Toss the dressing with the chilled vegetables.

To serve, remove and discard the string, and thinly slice the turkey. Spoon some sauce on the turkey slices, and pass remaining sauce separately. Garnish each plate with some of the marinated vegetables.

NOTE The dish and the sauce can be made up to 2 days in advance and refrigerated, tightly covered.

White Bean Soup
with Prosciutto and Spinach

*This is my all-time favorite bean soup, with flecks of salty prosciutto and bits of bright green
spinach in a thick and flavorful base of beans and other vegetables. It's hearty and filling,
and all it needs is a crusty loaf of bread and a tossed salad to make it a complete meal.*

SERVES **4 to 6**

SIZE **Medium slow cooker (4 or 5 quarts)**

TIME **Minimum of 4½ hours**

Prosciutto has been made for
more than 2,000 years in the
region of Italy near Parma,
and must come from Parma,
San Daniele, or the Veneto
to be authentic. If you've
wondered why prosciutto
seems to go so well with
Parmesan cheese, it might
be because the whey from
Parmigiano Reggiano is one
of the foods that is fed to
the pigs destined to become
prosciutto.

1½ cups dried navy beans or other
    small dried white beans
3 tablespoons olive oil
1 large onion, diced
1 medium carrot, chopped
1 celery rib, chopped
2 garlic cloves, minced
1 (14.5-ounce) can diced
    tomatoes, drained
⅓ pound prosciutto, diced
5 cups Chicken Stock (page 30) or
    store-bought stock

3 tablespoons chopped fresh
    parsley
2 tablespoons chopped fresh
    rosemary
6 ounces baby spinach
Salt and freshly ground black
    pepper, to taste
Freshly grated Parmesan cheese,
    for serving

Rinse the beans in a colander and place them in a mixing bowl
covered with cold salted water. Allow the beans to soak for a
minimum of 6 hours or overnight. Or place the beans into a
saucepan of salted water and bring to a boil over high heat. Boil
1 minute. Turn off the heat, cover the pan, and soak the beans for
1 hour. Drain the beans, discard the soaking water, rinse them well,
and cook or refrigerate the beans as soon as possible.

(continued on the following page)

(continued from the previous page)

Heat the olive oil in the slow cooker using the browning function or in a medium skillet over medium-high heat. Add the onion, carrot, and celery, and cook, stirring frequently, for 2 minutes. Add the garlic and cook for 1 minute, or until the onion is translucent. Scrape the mixture into the slow cooker, if using a skillet.

Add the drained beans, tomatoes, prosciutto, stock, parsley, and rosemary to the slow cooker, and stir well. Cook on low for 8 to 10 hours or on high for 4 to 5 hours, or until the beans are tender.

Using a slotted spoon, transfer half of the solids to a food processor fitted with a steel blade, or to a blender, and puree until smooth. Stir the puree back into the soup, add the spinach, and stir well. Cook on high for 20 to 30 minutes, or until the soup is simmering. Season with salt and pepper, and serve hot, passing around the Parmesan cheese separately.

NOTE The soup can be prepared up to 3 days in advance and refrigerated, tightly covered. Reheat it, covered, over low heat, stirring occasionally.

VARIATION

✳ **Substitute Swiss chard** for the spinach; the cooking time will remain the same.

Sauerbraten Stew

Sauerbraten is the quintessential German comfort food, and it can also be cooked as a stew with lots of vegetables to make the meal complete. Thickening the sauce with crushed gingersnap cookies intensifies the flavor, as well as giving it a pleasing texture.

SERVES **6 to 8**

SIZE **Medium slow cooker (4 or 5 quarts)**

MARINATING **time Minimum of 8 hours**

COOKING TIME **Minimum of 4 hours**

In this recipe, the marinade becomes the braising liquid, and as such, is subjected to high heat so there is no danger of contamination. As a general rule, never use a marinade raw. Either discard it or bring it to a boil for at least 5 minutes before using it.

NOTE The stew can be prepared up to 2 days in advance and refrigerated, tightly covered. Reheat it, covered, in a 350°F oven for 20 to 25 minutes, or until hot.

1 cup dry red wine
1 cup Beef Stock (page 29) or store-bought stock
½ cup red wine vinegar
2 tablespoons tomato paste
2 tablespoons Worcestershire sauce
1 tablespoon Dijon mustard
½ teaspoon ground allspice
½ teaspoon ground ginger
¼ cup firmly packed dark brown sugar
1 onion, thinly sliced
3 garlic cloves, minced
2 pounds beef chuck, cut into 1½-inch cubes
10 gingersnap cookies, crushed
3 large redskin potatoes, cut into 1½-inch cubes
2 carrots, cut into 1-inch pieces
2 parsnips, cut into 1-inch pieces
Salt and freshly ground black pepper, to taste

Combine the wine, stock, vinegar, tomato paste, Worcestershire sauce, mustard, allspice, ginger, and brown sugar in a heavy resealable plastic bag. Mix well, and add the onion, garlic, and beef. Marinate and refrigerate for 8 to 24 hours, turning the bag occasionally so the meat marinates evenly.

Transfer the beef and marinade to the slow cooker, and stir in the crushed gingersnaps, potatoes, carrots, and parsnips.

Cook on low for 8 to 10 hours or on high for 4 to 5 hours, or until the beef is very tender. Remove as much grease as possible from the surface of the sauce with a soup ladle. Season with salt and pepper, and serve.

Pork Carnitas

The slow cooker is a perfect way to get pork carnitas that are meltingly tender—and if you pop the meat under the broiler briefly you'll also give them the wonderful crispy edges that are associated with this dish. You can use a wide variety of toppings for carnitas. I usually serve them with a plate of thinly sliced jicama, sprinkled with lime juice as a side dish.

SERVES **4 to 6**

SIZE **Medium slow cooker (4 or 5 quarts)**

TIME **Minimum of 4 hours**

Some ingredients on the market add a natural smoky flavor to foods without adding chemicals. The two I use the most frequently are smoked Spanish paprika, sold as pimientón de la vera, in which the peppers are smoked over oak before they are ground, and there's a smoky nuance to chipotle peppers, because they are smoked jalapeños.

Vegetable oil spray
- 1 (2- to 2½-pound) boneless pork butt roast
- 1 juice orange
- 1 lime
- 1 small onion, diced
- ⅓ cup tomato juice or Bloody Mary mix
- 3 garlic cloves, minced
- 2 tablespoons smoked Spanish paprika
- 1 tablespoon ground cumin
- 1 tablespoon dried oregano, preferably Mexican
- 1 to 2 chipotle chiles in adobo sauce, finely chopped
- 1 bay leaf
- Salt and freshly ground black pepper, to taste
- 2 tablespoons olive oil
- 12 to 16 (6-inch) corn tortillas, warmed

TOPPINGS
- ¾ cup shredded green cabbage or iceberg lettuce
- ½ cup shredded Monterey Jack or jalapeño Jack cheese
- 1 avocado, thinly sliced
- ⅓ cup firmly packed fresh cilantro leaves
- ⅓ cup chopped red onion

Spray the inside of the slow cooker insert with vegetable oil spray. Cut the pork into 2-inch chunks. Cut the zest off the orange and lime with a vegetable peeler or sharp paring knife in thick strips and then squeeze out the juice from each fruit, discarding the seeds.

Combine the pork, orange zest, orange juice, lime zest, lime juice, onion, tomato juice, garlic, smoked paprika, cumin, oregano, chiles, and bay leaf in the slow cooker. Season with salt and pepper.

Cook on low for 8 to 10 hours or on high for 4 to 5 hours, or until the meat falls apart when speared by a fork. Drain the pork in a colander, reserving the cooking juices. Remove and discard the bay leaf and strips of citrus zest. Shred the meat with a meat fork.

Preheat the oven broiler and line a sheet pan with heavy-duty aluminum foil. Spread the pork out on top of the foil, and drizzle it with ½ cup of the cooking juices and the olive oil. Broil the pork 6 inches from the broiler element for 3 to 5 minutes, or until the top of the pork layer is browned and crispy. Remove the pork from the broiler, stir it, and moisten it with some of the remaining cooking juices.

To serve, mound the pork into the tortillas and pass around bowls of shredded cabbage, cheese, avocado, cilantro, and onion.

NOTE The carnitas can be cooked up to 2 days in advance and refrigerated, tightly covered. Reheat over low heat or in a microwave oven, and broil it just before serving.

VARIATION

∗ **Substitute boneless skinless chicken thighs,** cut into 2-inch pieces, for the pork. Cook the chicken on low for 6 to 8 hours and on high for 3 to 4 hours.

Smoked Sausages with Braised Red Cabbage and Butternut Squash

This dish is emblematic of fall to me, with its savory spices and the smoky nuance of the sausages that meld with the silky red cabbage and luscious butternut squash. Serve it with a side dish of crunchy coleslaw, made with fresh fennel, to balance all the flavors and textures.

SERVES **4 to 6**

SIZE **Medium slow cooker (4 or 5 quarts)**

TIME **Minimum of 3 hours**

It's important to sprinkle the red cabbage with the vinegar and sugar because that's what keeps it red while it cooks. Otherwise, the cabbage will turn purple. This dish is seasoned only at the end of the cooking time, because the amount of salt and pepper in sausages varies so widely.

1¼ pounds pork or chicken smoked sausage, such as kielbasa
3 tablespoons unsalted butter, divided
1 medium onion, chopped
1 Golden Delicious apple, peeled and chopped
1 (2-pound) red cabbage, cored and shredded
2 tablespoons red wine vinegar
2 tablespoons granulated sugar

1 pound peeled butternut squash, cut into 1-inch cubes
¾ cup dry red wine
½ cup Chicken Stock (page 30) or store-bought stock
1 (3-inch) cinnamon stick
1 bay leaf
1 tablespoon fresh thyme leaves
⅓ cup red currant jelly
Salt and freshly ground black pepper, to taste

Cut the sausages into 2-inch pieces and prick them with the tines of a fork. Heat 2 tablespoons of the butter in the slow cooker using the browning function or in a skillet over medium heat. Brown the sausages on all sides, then remove them from the pan with tongs, and set aside.

Add the onion and apple, and cook, stirring frequently, for 3 minutes, or until the onion is translucent. Scrape the mixture into the slow cooker if using a skillet.

Rinse the cabbage and cut it into quarters. Discard the core from each quarter and shred the cabbage. Add the cabbage to the slow cooker, sprinkle with the vinegar and sugar, and toss with the onion and apple mixture. Add the cubed squash.

(continued on the following page)

(continued from the previous page)

Stir the wine, stock, cinnamon stick, bay leaf, and thyme into the slow cooker and bury the sausages in the vegetable mixture.

Cook on low for 6 to 8 hours or on high for 3 to 4 hours or until cabbage is almost tender. If cooking on low, raise the heat to high. Remove and discard the cinnamon stick and bay leaf, and stir the jelly and remaining butter into the vegetable mixture. Cook on high for an additional 30 to 40 minutes, or until the cabbage is tender and glazed. Season with salt and pepper, and serve immediately.

NOTE The dish can be prepared up to 2 days in advance and refrigerated, tightly covered. Reheat it in a 350°F oven for 20 minutes, or until hot.

Eastern European Beef with Dried Fruits

(*Tsimmis*)

Sweet and sour is a popular combination around the world, and the way it's achieved in this richly flavored beef stew is by using dried fruit. Tsimmis is a traditional dish served by Eastern European Jews, and the word is also used in Yiddish: "What's the big tsimmis" means "What's the big deal?"

SERVES 6 to 8

SIZE Large slow cooker (7 quarts)

TIME Minimum of 5 hours

It's not only easy to make your own crystallized ginger (also called candied ginger), but as a result you get an intense, ginger-flavored simple syrup that can be used as a sweetener for drinks. Peel and slice 1 pound of fresh ginger root, about ⅛ inch thick; this is easy and fast to do using a mandoline. Cover the ginger with water, add a pinch of salt, and boil it for 30 minutes. Drain the ginger, reserving ½ cup of the water. Then place the ginger, reserved water, and 2 cups of sugar back in the saucepan and simmer it for 35 to 40 minutes, or until it registers 225°F on a candy thermometer. Transfer the slices to a cooling rack and allow them to sit for 2 hours; pour off and reserve the syrup. Toss the slices with additional sugar and allow them to sit overnight.

2 pounds boneless short ribs or chuck roast, cut into 2-inch cubes
1½ pounds carrots, peeled and cut into ½-inch slices
1½ pounds sweet potatoes peeled and cut into 1-inch cubes
1 large onion, diced
1 cup dried apricots
1 cup pitted prunes
1 cup apple cider
1 cup Beef Stock (page 29) or store-bought stock
2 tablespoons minced crystallized ginger
½ teaspoon freshly grated nutmeg
½ teaspoon ground cinnamon
Salt and freshly ground black pepper, to taste
⅓ cup chopped fresh parsley, for serving

Preheat the oven broiler, and line a broiler pan with heavy-duty aluminum foil. Brown the short ribs for 3 to 5 minutes per side, or until lightly browned. Transfer the beef to the slow cooker.

Add the carrots, sweet potatoes, onion, apricots, and prunes to the slow cooker. Combine the cider, stock, crystallized ginger, nutmeg, and cinnamon in a mixing bowl, and pour the mixture into the slow cooker.

(continued on the following page)

(continued from the previous page)

Cook on low for 10 to 12 hours or on high for 5 to 6 hours, or until the carrots and beef are very tender. Remove as much grease as possible from the surface of the stew with a soup ladle. Season with salt and pepper, and serve immediately, sprinkling each serving with parsley.

NOTE The dish can be prepared up to 2 days in advance and refrigerated, tightly covered. Reheat it, covered, in a 350°F oven for 10 to 25 minutes, or until hot.

VARIATION

* **Substitute cubes of boneless veal stew meat** for the beef and reduce the cooking time to 8 to 10 hours on low or 4 to 5 hours on high.

chapter 3

The Dutch Oven

Few pots are as versatile as the Dutch oven. You can use it to simmer a dish on top of the stove, or start it on a burner and then transfer it to the oven to finish cooking unattended. You can also use a Dutch oven to boil, bake, fry, and roast.

The Dutch oven is hardly a new kid on the block; it's been in use since the seventeenth century. In English-speaking countries other than the United States it is called a *casserole*—which means "saucepan" in French—and it's called a *cocotte* in France. A Dutch oven has relatively low straight sides, a wide diameter, and a tight-fitting lid.

The reason it's called a Dutch oven is that the process for forming molds for cooking vessels using dry sand was developed in the Netherlands. This gave the pots made in that country a smoother surface than those made in England and other European nations.

Dutch ovens come in both round and oval shapes, and I have a real bias for round ones; oval-shaped pots hang off the sides of even large burners. In terms of size, you want one that has a capacity of either 6 or 7 quarts. They are usually made from enameled cast iron, which conducts and retains heat well and is easy to clean.

Dutch ovens are known for being heavy—a 7-quart Dutch oven can weigh up to 17 pounds, and that's before you put anything into it. Some Dutch ovens are made from enameled aluminum, which is relatively as light as a proverbial feather when compared to cast iron. But the aluminum pots have a tendency to scorch food and can dent easily.

Because Dutch ovens are hefty, always look for one with large handles that are easy to grip. Although a rainbow of colors is available for the exterior of the pots (to match just about any kitchen décor), you should buy one with a light-colored interior so that you can monitor the progress of food while it is browning.

Another factor to consider is the cost, although one should regard a Dutch oven as a lifetime investment. Most professional chefs and cookbook authors say the gold standard for a Dutch oven is Le Creuset®, a pan imported from France that sells for more than $350. Many domestic pots are available, however, including one by Lodge®, a leader in cast iron cookery, that sells for less than $100.

While there's no technique involved in using a Dutch oven, you should be careful when pulling one out of the oven: always bend your knees and lift it out gently.

Acorn Squash and Farro Stew

Farro, an ancient form of wheat native to the Mediterranean region, has been experiencing a spike in popularity for a few years now. Farro contains lots of fiber, even in its semi-pearled and quick-to-cook forms. In addition, nutritionists tout it as a source of B vitamins, zinc, iron, and a good dose of protein. Farro also has a nutty flavor and a pleasing texture that pair wonderfully with sweet winter squash.

SERVES **4 to 6**

SIZE **6- to 7-quart Dutch oven**

TIME **35 to 40 minutes**

Like rice, there are various species of farro, and also like rice, cooking time depends on how the grain has been processed. Hulled farro is the whole grain in its most nutritious form, because it hasn't been processed. Hulled farro really needs to be soaked overnight in cold water, however, because even after a few hours of cooking you'll find that the interior of the grains remains hard and almost inedible. I use semi-pearled farro, sometimes called *semiperlato*. This form of the grain still has plenty of nutty flavor and nutrition, but the kernels have been processed to remove some of the bran, so no soaking is needed, and it cooks in about 30 to 40 minutes in a Dutch oven.

NOTE The farro can be prepared up to 2 days in advance and refrigerated, tightly covered. Reheat it covered at 325°F for 15 to 20 minutes, or until hot.

2 tablespoons unsalted butter
1 tablespoon vegetable oil
1 large sweet onion, such as Vidalia or Bermuda, diced
2 garlic cloves, minced
1 tablespoon fresh thyme leaves
2 cups semi-pearled farro, rinsed well
3½ cups Vegetable Stock (page 33), Chicken Stock (page 30), or store-bought stock
Salt and freshly ground black pepper, to taste
1 pound peeled acorn or butternut squash, cut into 2-inch cubes
½ cup freshly grated Parmesan cheese, for serving (optional)

Preheat the oven to 350°F.

Heat the butter and oil in the Dutch oven over medium-high heat. Add the onion and cook, stirring frequently, for 5 minutes, or until it softens and starts to brown. Add the garlic and thyme and cook for 1 minute, stirring constantly.

Stir in the farro and the stock, season with salt and pepper, and lay the squash cubes on top of the farro. Bring the liquid to a boil on top of the stove and transfer the pan to the oven. Bake, covered, for 30 to 35 minutes, or until the farro and squash are tender.

Serve immediately, passing around the cheese separately, if using.

Couscous with Vegetables and Dried Fruit

Dried fruit is used extensively in North African cooking, and it adds a lush sweetness to balance the savory vegetables and spices in this easy-to-make vegetarian stew.

SERVES **6 to 8**

SIZE **6- to 7-quart Dutch oven**

TIME **1¼ hours**

You might think it's a waste to discard the ingredients that simmer with the broth, but it's not. Their purpose is to create a more intensely flavored stock. In classic French cooking, the resulting product is called a *court bouillon*, and it's used to poach foods such as chicken and fish.

- 5 cups Vegetable Stock (page 33), Chicken Stock, (page 30), or store-bought stock
- 3 tablespoons olive oil, divided
- 6 large fresh cilantro springs
- 6 garlic cloves, peeled
- 3 (3-inch) cinnamon sticks
- 2 tablespoons ground cumin
- 1½ tablespoons curry powder or garam masala
- 4 leeks, white part only, halved lengthwise, and cut into 1-inch lengths
- 4 medium carrots, halved lengthwise, and cut into 1-inch pieces
- 2 russet potatoes, peeled and cut into eighths
- ½ pound small white turnips, quartered
- 3 small onions, peeled and halved
- 3 cups whole-wheat couscous
- Salt and freshly ground black pepper, to taste
- 2 medium zucchini, ends trimmed, halved lengthwise, and cut into 1-inch lengths
- 3 ripe large tomatoes, cored, seeded, and cut into sixths
- 1 (15-ounce) can garbanzo beans, drained and rinsed
- 1 cup pitted prunes, halved
- ½ cup dried currants
- ¼ cup chopped fresh cilantro (optional)

Combine the stock, 2 tablespoons of the oil, cilantro sprigs, garlic, cinnamon sticks, cumin, and curry powder in a Dutch oven. Bring to a boil over high heat, reduce the heat to low, and simmer, uncovered, for 30 minutes. Strain the stock, pressing with the back of a spoon to extract as much liquid as possible. Discard the solids, and return the stock to the pan.

Add the leeks, carrots, potatoes, turnips, and onions to the stock. Bring to a boil over high heat, reduce the heat to low, and simmer, uncovered, for 30 minutes.

Combine the couscous, remaining oil, and 3 cups very hot tap water in a mixing bowl. Season with salt and pepper, stir well, and set aside.

Add the zucchini, tomatoes, garbanzo beans, prunes, and dried currants to the Dutch oven. Simmer, uncovered, for an additional 15 minutes. Stir in the cilantro, if using, and season with salt and pepper. Spoon the couscous into shallow bowls and top with the vegetables and broth. Serve immediately.

NOTE The vegetable mixture can be prepared up to 3 days in advance and refrigerated, tightly covered. Bring it to a boil over medium heat before serving.

Peruvian Vegetable and Quinoa Stew

Quinoa has sprinted to the front of the grain gang because it's gluten-free, cooks quickly, and contains more nutrients than white rice. It's almost nutty flavor takes well to myriad seasonings, as in this savory stew with a rainbow of vegetables.

SERVES **4 to 6**

SIZE **6- to 7-quart Dutch oven**

TIME **30 to 32 minutes**

Quinoa comes in three main colors—red, white, and black. Nutritionally they're the same, but they cook at a slightly different rate. I recommend red quinoa for this stew, both because of its color and because I think it holds its shape better than the more common white variety. Although red quinoa takes a bit longer to cook than white quinoa, the visually dramatic black quinoa takes the longest time of all. But these time differences, measured in just minutes, are minor, so pick whatever color you like.

1 cup red quinoa
2 ears fresh corn
2 tablespoons olive oil
1 medium red onion, diced
1 orange or red bell pepper, seeds and ribs removed, diced
3 garlic cloves, minced
1 tablespoon smoked Spanish paprika
1 tablespoon ground coriander
2 teaspoons ground cumin
6 cups Vegetable Stock (page 33) or store-bought stock

1 pound redskin potatoes, cut into ¾-inch pieces
Salt and freshly ground black pepper, to taste
1 medium zucchini, diced
3 ripe plum tomatoes, cored, seeded, and diced
¼ pound *queso fresco*, crumbled, for serving
1 avocado, diced, for serving
½ cup chopped fresh cilantro, for serving

Place the quinoa in a strainer and rinse it well under cold running water. Set aside. Cut the kernels off the corn, reserving the cobs.

Heat the oil in the Dutch oven over medium heat. Add the onion and bell pepper and cook, stirring frequently, for 5 to 6 minutes, or until the vegetables soften. Stir in the garlic, paprika, coriander, and cumin, and cook, stirring constantly, for 30 seconds.

Stir in the stock and potatoes, season with salt and pepper, and add the corncobs. Bring to a boil over high heat, and then reduce the heat to low and simmer the mixture for 10 minutes. Remove and discard the corncobs and stir in the quinoa.

(continued on the following page)

(continued from the previous page)

Bring the mixture back to a boil and simmer for 8 minutes. Add the zucchini and tomatoes and cook for 5 minutes, then add the corn kernels and cook for an additional 2 minutes.

Adjust the seasoning and ladle the stew into low bowls, topping each serving with *queso fresco*, avocado, and cilantro. Serve immediately.

NOTE The stew can be made up to 2 days in advance and refrigerated, tightly covered. Reheat it over low heat, adding more stock as needed, because the stew thickens as it sits.

VARIATION

∗ Add 1 pound of boneless, skinless chicken thighs, cut into 1-inch pieces, to the Dutch oven along with the onion and bell pepper, and substitute chicken stock for the vegetable stock.

Herbed Clams
with Linguine and Bacon

The sweetness of leeks and shallots and the smoky nuances in the sauce, thanks to the bacon, perfectly complement the briny goodness of clams, combined with assorted herbs and a touch of tomato. If you like linguine with clam sauce, you'll go bonkers for this dish; the pasta has such a depth of flavor because it's cooked in clam juice instead of water.

SERVES **4 to 6**

SIZE **6- to 7-quart Dutch oven**

TIME **20 minutes**

Mollusks, like fresh clams and mussels, need to go through a process called *purging*, which makes them "spit out" any grit from inside their shells, before you cook them. The result: tender mollusks that don't taste as if you're chewing on sandpaper. To purge the mollusks, scrub them well and then place them in a bowl of cold tap water and stir in a bit of salt. Then sprinkle cornmeal over the top of the water and allow the mollusks to sit for 30 to 45 minutes. Remove them from the water, and rinse them again. The purging can be done up to 6 hours before you plan to cook clams or mussels. Refrigerate them, covered with a damp paper towel.

- 2 to 3 dozen littleneck clams
- 1 teaspoon kosher salt
- 1 tablespoon cornmeal
- ¼ pound bacon, cut into thin slices
- 1 cup sliced leeks, white and pale green parts, rinsed well
- 2 shallots, sliced
- 3 garlic cloves, minced
- ½ cup dry white wine
- Pinch of crushed red pepper flakes
- 1 (8-ounce) bottle clam juice
- 12 to 16 ounces fresh linguine
- 1 cup cherry tomatoes, halved
- 2 tablespoons chopped fresh parsley
- 2 tablespoons chopped fresh basil
- 1 tablespoon chopped fresh marjoram or oregano
- Freshly ground black pepper, to taste
- ½ cup freshly grated Parmesan cheese, for serving (optional)

Scrub the clams well under cold running water with a clean metal brush. Place them in a mixing bowl of cold tap water, stir in the salt, and sprinkle the cornmeal over the top. Allow the clams to sit for 30 to 45 minutes, and then scoop them out of the bowl with a slotted spoon. Rinse them again. Then rinse out the mixing bowl and place the clams in it.

Heat the Dutch oven over medium-high heat and add the bacon. Cook the bacon for 4 to 6 minutes, or until it's almost crisp. Add the leeks and shallots to the Dutch oven and cook for 3 minutes, or until the leeks are translucent. Add the garlic and cook for 1 minute, stirring constantly. Add the wine and crushed red pepper flakes to the pan and cook over high heat for 2 minutes.

(continued on the following page)

(continued from the previous page)

Add the clams to the Dutch oven, cover the pan, and cook for 3 to 5 minutes, or until the clams steam open. Remove the clams from the pan with tongs, and set them aside, covered lightly with foil. Discard any clams that did not open.

Add the clam juice, linguine, tomatoes, parsley, basil, and marjoram (or oregano) to the pan. Cook the pasta for 2 to 3 minutes, or until al dente. Depending on the number of clams, you may need to add up to ½ cup water to create enough liquid to cook the pasta.

Return the clams to the pan to reheat. Then divide the mixture into shallow bowls, season with pepper, and serve immediately. Pass around the cheese separately, if using.

NOTE This dish should be prepared just before serving it. If there are leftovers, remove the clams from the shells, refrigerate the pasta tightly covered, and reheat the leftovers in a microwave oven.

North Beach Cioppino

Cioppino is San Francisco's answer to French bouillabaisse; it's a fish stew made in a richly flavored tomato sauce. I serve it over thick slices of toast, along with a green salad, as the perfect foil.

SERVES **4 to 6**

SIZE **6- to 7-quart Dutch oven**

TIME **30 to 35 minutes**

When serving a fish stew, I usually give guests multiple utensils. Of course you need a soup spoon for the broth, but I also give them a knife, fork, and shellfish fork, too. Prying the nugget of meat from a mussel shell can be difficult, and some diners like to cut up the toast with a knife and fork before enjoying it.

- 1 pound live mussels
- 3 tablespoons olive oil
- 1 large onion, diced
- 1 small fennel bulb, rinsed, trimmed, cored, and diced
- 2 carrots, sliced
- 3 garlic cloves, minced
- 1 cup dry red wine
- 2 cups Seafood Stock (page 32) or store-bought stock
- 1 (28-ounce) can crushed tomatoes in tomato puree
- 2 tablespoons chopped fresh parsley
- 1 tablespoon fresh thyme leaves
- 2 teaspoons fennel seeds, crushed
- 1 bay leaf
- ½ teaspoon crushed red pepper flakes, or to taste
- 1 pound thick white firm-fleshed fish fillets, such as cod, halibut, or swordfish, rinsed and cut into 1-inch cubes
- 1 pound (21 to 25 per pound) shrimp, peeled and deveined
- Salt and freshly ground black pepper, to taste
- 4 to 6 (¾-inch-thick) slices toasted ciabatta or Italian bread, for serving

Clean the mussels by scrubbing them well with a brush under cold water; discard any that are not tightly shut. Scrape off any barnacles with a knife. If the beard is still attached, remove it by pulling it from tip to hinge, or by pulling and cutting it off with a knife. Refrigerate the mussels, covered by a damp paper towel.

Heat the oil in the Dutch oven medium-high heat. Add the onion, fennel, and carrots, and cook, stirring frequently, for 2 minutes. Add the garlic and cook for 1 minute, or until the onion is translucent. Add the wine, and cook for 3 minutes.

Add the stock, tomatoes, parsley, thyme, fennel seeds, bay leaf, and crushed red pepper flakes to the pot. Bring the mixture to a boil over medium-high heat, stirring occasionally. Reduce the heat to low, and simmer the stew, covered, for 15 to 20 minutes, or until the vegetables soften.

Add the mussels to the pan, cover the pan, and bring to a boil over high heat. Steam the mussels for 3 minutes, and stir to redistribute the seafood. Add the fish and shrimp, cover the pan again, and cook for 3 to 5 minutes, or until the fish is cooked and flakes easily. Discard any mussels that did not open.

Remove and discard the bay leaf, and season the stew with salt and pepper. Serve immediately, spooning the stew over a thick slice of toast.

NOTE The soup base can be prepared up to 2 days in advance and refrigerated, tightly covered. Reheat it, covered, over low heat, stirring frequently until it comes to a boil, and then cook the mussels and the fish.

VARIATION

∗ Substitute white wine for the red wine, and substitute ½ cup of freshly squeezed orange juice for ½ cup of the seafood stock.

Greek Chicken with Orzo

The combination of tart lemon and aromatic oregano is part and parcel of Greek cuisine, and here it flavors the orzo in this easy chicken dish. The tomatoes add succulence as well as color, and a sprinkling of feta cheese at the end brings it all together.

SERVES **4 to 6**

SIZE **6- to 7-quart Dutch oven**

TIME **35 minutes**

Gardeners have been cultivating different species of basil for decades and clearly grasp the variations in flavor, and the same is true of plants lumped under the name of oregano. The most pungent of these is Greek oregano, which also has the strongest flavor and can be found in supermarkets. Italian oregano, which is omnipresent in pizza parlors, is actually a hybrid of oregano and sweet marjoram, which gives it a milder taste. Mexican oregano, sometimes called Puerto Rican oregano, is a member of a different genus; it's related to lemon verbena and has a strong aroma when added to dishes.

1 **lemon**
2 **cups orzo**
4 **to 6 bone-in, skin-on chicken pieces of your choice (breasts cut in half, thighs, legs)**
Salt and freshly ground black pepper, to taste
3 **tablespoons olive oil, divided**
1 **medium onion, diced**
4 **garlic cloves, minced**
2 **teaspoons paprika**
1 **tablespoon dried oregano, preferably Greek**
1 **pint cherry or grape tomatoes, halved**
3 **cups Chicken Stock (page 30) or store-bought stock**
2 **bay leaves**
¼ **cup chopped pitted Kalamata olives**
2 **tablespoons chopped fresh parsley**
½ **cup crumbled feta cheese**

Grate the zest off the lemon and squeeze out the juice. Set aside.

Place the Dutch oven over medium-high heat. Add the orzo and toast it, stirring frequently, for 3 minutes or until lightly browned. Scrape the orzo into a bowl and set aside.

Pat the chicken dry with paper towels and sprinkle the pieces with salt and pepper. Heat 2 tablespoons of the oil in the Dutch oven over medium-high heat. Add the chicken pieces, being careful not to crowd the pan. Brown the pieces well on all sides, turning them gently with tongs. Remove the chicken from the pan and set it aside.

Add the remaining oil to the Dutch oven. Add the onion and cook, stirring frequently, for 3 minutes, or until the onion is translucent. Stir in the garlic, paprika, and oregano and cook for 30 seconds, stirring constantly.

Return the chicken to the pan, and add the lemon zest, lemon juice, tomatoes, stock, bay leaves, and olives. Bring to a boil, reduce the heat to low, and simmer the chicken, covered, for 20 minutes. Add the orzo to the Dutch oven, stir well, and cook for 10 to 12 minutes, or until the orzo is al dente and the chicken is cooked through and no longer pink.

Remove and discard the bay leaves, season with salt and pepper, and serve immediately, garnishing each serving with parsley and a sprinkling of feta.

NOTE The dish can be prepared up to 2 days in advance and refrigerated, tightly covered. Reheat it, covered, in a 350°F oven for 20 to 25 minutes, or until hot. Add additional stock if the orzo seems dry.

Coq au Vin

Real coq au vin is made from an old rooster, which is why authentic recipes require braising the beast for a few hours. It's almost impossible to find even a stewing chicken these days, so this recipe is made with the usual chicken parts. However, adding the white meat later in the cooking process keeps it from drying out. And of course a red wine, preferably from Burgundy, is the best choice of beverage.

SERVES **4 to 6**

SIZE **6- to 7-quart Dutch oven**

MARINATING TIME **A minimum of 4 hours but preferably overnight**

COOKING TIME **1½ hours**

Part of silky texture in a dish like coq au vin comes from the natural gelatin that used to be found in homemade stocks when they were made from gelatinous bones or chicken feet. Adding some gelatin to the dish replicates that aspect. It's important to sprinkle the gelatin on cold liquid to soften it, because if you just pour it in, some granules may not melt properly.

- 2 cups dry red wine
- 2 teaspoons kosher salt
- Freshly ground black pepper, to taste
- 3 tablespoons chopped fresh parsley
- 1 tablespoon chopped fresh thyme leaves
- 3 garlic cloves, minced
- 1 bay leaf
- 4 to 6 bone-in, skin-on chicken pieces of your choice (breasts cut in half, thighs, legs)
- 2 (¼-ounce) packets unflavored gelatin
- 1½ cups Chicken Stock (page 30) or store-bought stock, cold
- ¼ pound thick-sliced bacon, cut into ¾-inch pieces
- 1 large onion, diced
- ½ pound cremini mushrooms, trimmed and halved, if large
- 3 tablespoons all-purpose flour
- 2 carrots, thickly sliced
- 1 to 1¼ pounds Yukon gold potatoes, cut into 2-inch chunks
- 1 tablespoon tomato paste
- 10 ounces frozen pearl onions, thawed

Combine the wine, salt, pepper, parsley, thyme, garlic, and bay leaf in a heavy resealable plastic bag. Add the chicken pieces and marinate the chicken, refrigerated, for a minimum of 4 hours, but preferably overnight.

Sprinkle the gelatin over the cold stock and set aside to soften.

Heat the Dutch oven over medium-high heat. Cook the bacon for 5 to 7 minutes, or until crisp. Remove the bacon from the pan with a slotted spoon, and drain on paper towels. Set aside. Add the diced onions and mushrooms to the pan and cook for 3 minutes, or until the onion is translucent. Remove the vegetables from the pan and set aside.

Remove the chicken pieces from the marinade, reserving the marinade. Pat the chicken with paper towels, and brown it in the Dutch oven, being careful not to crowd the pan. Remove the chicken pieces from the pan.

Preheat the oven to 350°F.

Stir the flour into the Dutch oven and cook, stirring constantly, for 1 minute, or until the mixture turns slightly beige, is bubbly, and appears to have grown in volume. Add the reserved marinade and bring to a boil over medium-high heat. Boil until the wine is reduced by one-fourth. Stir in the stock and bring back to a boil.

Return the chicken thighs and legs to the Dutch oven as well as the bacon, onion, and mushrooms, and then add the carrots, potato cubes, and tomato paste. Bring to a boil, then transfer the Dutch oven to the oven and bake for 45 minutes, uncovered.

Add the chicken breast pieces and pearl onions to the Dutch oven and bake for an additional 30 minutes, uncovered, or until all the chicken is cooked through and no longer pink. Remove and discard the bay leaf, season with salt and pepper, and serve.

NOTE The dish can be made up to 2 days in advance and refrigerated, tightly covered. Reheat it over low heat or in a 350°F oven for 20 to 30 minutes, or until hot.

Moroccan Chicken Tagine

The flavors in this dish just dance in your mouth. You've got salty olives, sweet caramelized onions, and a double dose of tart lemon enlivening each bite. Serve it with some flatbread and a tossed salad.

SERVES **4 to 6**

SIZE **6- to 7-quart Dutch oven**

TIME **1 hour**

Few ingredients are as easy to make as preserved lemons, a mainstay of North African cooking that deliver a really assertive dose of lemony tartness. To make them you need lemons, salt, sugar, and a lot of patience. For eight whole lemons you'll need ½ cup kosher salt and ¼ cup granulated sugar. Cut the lemons into quarters, keeping them connected at the base. Toss them with salt and sugar and refrigerate them overnight. The next day pack them into a sterilized canning jar, pressing them down so they are submerged in liquid that seeped out from the marinating. Then seal the jar and leave them alone for a minimum of 2 weeks, although they'll be good for 6 to 8 months if kept in the liquid.

- 2 large or 4 small preserved lemons
- 4 to 6 bone-in, skin-on chicken pieces of your choice (breasts cut in half, thighs, legs)
- Salt and freshly ground black pepper, to taste
- ¼ cup olive oil, divided
- 2 large sweet onions, such as Bermuda or Vidalia, thinly sliced
- 5 garlic cloves, minced
- 3 tablespoons all-purpose flour
- 2 teaspoons paprika
- 1½ teaspoons ground turmeric
- 1 teaspoon ground ginger
- 1 teaspoon ground cumin
- 1 (3-inch) cinnamon stick
- ¾ pound peeled butternut or acorn squash, cut into ¾-inch cubes
- 2 parsnips, thickly sliced
- ½ cup Kalamata olives, pitted and chopped
- 2 cups Chicken Stock (page 30) or store-bought stock
- ¼ cup freshly squeezed lemon juice
- 2 tablespoons chopped fresh cilantro, for serving

Halve the lemons, discard the pulp, and cut the rind into thin strips. Set aside.

Pat the chicken dry with paper towels and sprinkle the pieces with salt and pepper. Heat 2 tablespoons of the oil in the Dutch oven over medium-high heat. Add the chicken pieces, being careful not to crowd the pan. Brown the pieces well on all sides, turning them gently with tongs. Remove the chicken from the pan and set it aside.

Add the remaining oil to the Dutch oven along with the onions, tossing to coat them evenly. Cover the pan, reduce the heat to medium, and cook for 5 minutes. Uncover the pan, increase the heat to medium-high, and cook for 10 to 12 minutes, or until browned. Add the garlic, flour, paprika, turmeric, ginger, and cumin. Cook for 1 minute, stirring constantly.

Nestle the cinnamon stick among the onions, return the chicken to the pan, and add the lemon rind, squash, parsnips, olives, stock, and lemon juice. Bring to a boil, reduce the heat to low, and simmer the chicken, covered, for 30 minutes, or until the chicken is cooked through and no longer pink and the vegetables are tender. Remove and discard the cinnamon stick.

Serve immediately, sprinkling each serving with cilantro.

NOTE The chicken mixture can be prepared up to 2 days in advance and refrigerated, tightly covered. Reheat the mixture in the Dutch oven before topping it with the dumplings. Do not make the dumpling dough or cook the dumplings until just before serving.

Chicken with Herbed Cornmeal Dumplings

Dumplings are biscuits that are steamed rather than baked, and this recipe uses a precooked rotisserie chicken, so keep this dish in mind during the hot summer months when keeping the oven off is a goal. The aromatic creamy base of the stew is flavored with herbs, and the light and fluffy dumplings form a textural contrast as a crown. I usually serve this dish with crunchy coleslaw.

SERVES 4 to 6

SIZE 6- to 7-quart Dutch oven

TIME 25 to 30 minutes

Dumplings have been one of the world's peasant dishes since at least the seventeenth century, when the word was first recorded, but, according to food historian Alan Davidson, they probably predate that era by a few centuries. In the United States, they are most frequently associated with the Appalachian region and the South, but in other cultures it's common to serve steamed dumplings stuffed with fruit for dessert.

- 6 tablespoons (¾ stick) unsalted butter, divided
- 1 large onion, chopped
- 2 carrots, thinly sliced
- 2 celery ribs, thinly sliced
- 2 garlic cloves, minced
- ¼ cup dry white wine
- ½ cup plus 3 tablespoons all-purpose flour, divided
- 1 cup Chicken Stock (page 30) or store-bought stock
- 1 cup half-and-half
- 3 tablespoons chopped fresh parsley, divided
- 2 tablespoons chopped fresh sage, divided
- 1½ teaspoons fresh thyme leaves
- Salt and freshly ground black pepper, to taste
- 1 (3- to 4-pound) rotisserie chicken, skin and bones discarded and meat cut into 1-inch pieces
- 2 ounces fresh green beans, trimmed and cut into 1-inch pieces
- ½ cup coarse yellow cornmeal
- 1 teaspoon baking powder
- ¼ teaspoon baking soda
- Pinch of salt
- ½ cup whole buttermilk

Heat 2 tablespoons of the butter in the Dutch oven over medium-high heat. Add the onion, carrots, and celery, and cook, stirring frequently for 2 minutes. Add the garlic and cook for 1 minute, or until the onion is translucent. Add the wine and cook for 3 minutes, stirring occasionally, or until the wine is almost evaporated. Scrape the mixture into a mixing bowl.

Heat 2 tablespoons of the remaining butter in the Dutch oven over low heat. Stir in 3 tablespoons of the flour and cook, stirring constantly, for 2 minutes. Whisk in the stock and bring to a boil over medium-high heat, whisking constantly.

(continued on the following page)

(continued from the previous page)

Return the vegetables to the Dutch oven, stir in the half-and-half, 2 tablespoons of the parsley, 1 tablespoon of the sage, and the thyme, and simmer for 2 minutes. Season with salt and pepper and stir in the chicken and green beans.

While the mixture simmers, prepare the dumpling dough. Combine the remaining flour, cornmeal, baking powder, baking soda, and salt in a mixing bowl. Cut in the remaining butter with a pastry blender or your fingers until the mixture resembles coarse meal. Add the buttermilk, remaining parsley, and remaining sage. Stir with a fork until the dough is moistened.

Drop the dough by tablespoon amounts on top of the chicken, spacing the dough bits 1 inch apart. Cover the Dutch oven and cook over medium-low heat for 15 to 20 minutes, or until the dumplings are puffed and cooked through. *Do not uncover the Dutch oven while the dumplings are steaming.* Serve immediately.

NOTE The dish can be prepared up to 2 days in advance and refrigerated, tightly covered. Reheat it, covered, in a 350°F oven for 20 to 25 minutes, or until hot.

Kentucky Burgoo

While the bayous of Louisiana might be known as Gumbo Gulf, there's no question that the Appalachian Mountains in general and the state of Kentucky in particular are the "Burgoo Belt." In fact, this meat and vegetable stew is as popular as mint juleps at the Kentucky Derby. There are as many recipes and variations of burgoo as there are cooks, but this one was served to me at Forest Retreat, a famed horse farm in Carlisle, Kentucky. While recipes for burgoo may change, there is one constant: burgoo should always be served with cornbread, preferably right out of a cast iron skillet.

SERVES **6 to 8**

SIZE **6- to 7-quart Dutch oven**

TIME **2 hours**

The common wisdom has always been that foods like soups and stews taste better when they're reheated. But I don't agree, because reheating can demolish the texture and color of vegetables, such as the green beans and corn kernels in this recipe. What really takes the time to cook are the meats, so I suggest adding the quick-cooking vegetables only to the portion of the stew you plan to serve, and reserve the rest to add to the base when reheating it the next day.

2 pounds lamb shoulder chops
1½ pounds (about 4) chicken thighs with bones and skin
1 pound beef shank
Salt and freshly ground black pepper, to taste
3 tablespoons bacon grease or vegetable oil
1 large onion, diced
4 garlic cloves, minced
¼ cup all-purpose flour
3 cups Chicken Stock (page 30) or store-bought stock
3 cups Beef Stock (page 29) or store-bought stock
1 (14.5-ounce) can diced tomatoes, undrained
¼ cup Worcestershire sauce
¼ cup ketchup
2 tablespoons cider vinegar
3 large Yukon Gold potatoes, peeled and cut into ¾-inch chunks
1½ cups lima beans
1½ cups fresh corn kernels
3 ounces fresh green beans, stemmed and cut into 1-inch lengths
Hot red pepper sauce, to taste
Chopped fresh parsley, for serving

Pat the lamb chops, chicken thighs, and beef shank dry with paper towels, and sprinkle them with salt and pepper. Heat the bacon grease in the Dutch oven over medium-high heat. Brown the meats on all sides, being careful not to crowd the pan. Remove all the meats and set aside.

(continued on the following page)

(continued from the previous page)

Add the onion to the pan and cook for 2 minutes, add the garlic, and cook for 1 additional minute, or until the onion is translucent. Stir in the flour and cook, stirring constantly, for 1 minute, or until the mixture turns slightly beige, is bubbly, and appears to have grown in volume. Whisk in the chicken stock, beef stock, tomatoes, Worcestershire sauce, ketchup, and vinegar. Bring to a boil.

Add the lamb chops, chicken, and beef shank and simmer the meats for 30 minutes. Transfer the chicken to a plate with tongs, and when cool enough to handle, cut the meat into bite-sized pieces, discarding the skin and bones. Set aside. Continue to cook the lamb and beef for an additional 1 hour, or until they are tender. Transfer the lamb and the beef to a plate, and when cool enough to handle, cut the meat into bite-sized pieces, discarding any bones and gristle. Remove as much grease as possible from the surface of the stew with a soup ladle.

Add the potatoes and lima beans to the Dutch oven and cook for 15 minutes. Return the meats to the stew and add the corn and green beans. Cook for 5 minutes; then season the stew with salt, pepper, and hot red pepper sauce. Ladle the stew into bowls, sprinkling each serving with parsley.

NOTE The burgoo can be made up to 3 days in advance and refrigerated, tightly covered. Reheat it over low heat, covered, until it simmers before serving.

Caribbean Veal Stew

This is a vibrant dish loaded with ingredients from the sunny islands, including rum, which imbues the sauce with its heady flavor. There's a balance to the sweet and sour eating profile, and adding sugar snap peas at the end of the cooking time brings a crisp texture, too.

SERVES **6 to 8**

SIZE **6- to 7-quart Dutch oven**

MARINATING TIME **Minimum of 4 hours** COOKING TIME **2 hours**

I call for ground cloves in this recipe, but you can always substitute whole cloves. A teaspoon of ground cloves is the equivalent of 1½ teaspoons whole cloves. Like bay leaves, cloves should always be removed and discarded from a dish before it's served.

- ½ cup dark rum
- ½ cup Chicken Stock (page 30) or store-bought stock
- 1 tablespoon cider vinegar
- 1½ teaspoons dried oregano
- ¼ teaspoon ground cloves
- Salt and freshly ground black pepper, to taste
- ⅓ cup olive oil, divided
- 2 pounds lean veal stew meat, cut into 1½-inch pieces, patted dry with paper towels
- ¾ cup firmly packed dark brown sugar
- 1 (12-ounce) can lager beer
- 2 ounces (½ cup) diced ham
- ¼ cup chopped pimiento-stuffed green olives
- ¾ cup diced pitted prunes
- 3 carrots, cut into 1¾-inch chunks
- 3 large yams, cut into 2-inch chunks
- 1½ tablespoons cornstarch
- ½ pound sugar snap peas
- ⅓ cup chopped fresh cilantro, for serving

Combine the rum, stock, vinegar, oregano, cloves, salt, and pepper in heavy resealable plastic bag. Shake to dissolve the seasonings, add 1 tablespoon of the olive oil, and shake well again. Add the veal, push the air out of the bag, and marinate in the refrigerator for at least 4 hours and up to 12 hours, turning the bag occasionally.

Drain the marinade from the meat, reserving the marinade. Pat the veal dry with paper towels. Heat the remaining oil in the Dutch oven over medium-high heat. Add the veal to the Dutch oven, and cook, turning the pieces with tongs, until brown on all sides.

(continued on the following page)

(continued from the previous page)

Pour the reserved marinade into the pan, along with the brown sugar, beer, ham, olives, prunes, carrots, and yams. Bring to a boil over medium-high heat, then reduce the heat to low, cover the pan, and cook for 1¾ hours, or until the veal is tender.

Remove as much grease as possible from the surface of the sauce with a soup ladle. Combine the cornstarch and 2 tablespoons of cold water in a small cup. Bring the liquid back to a boil over medium-high heat. Stir the cornstarch mixture and sugar snap peas into the stew. Cook over medium heat for 2 minutes or until slightly thickened.

Adjust the seasoning and serve immediately, sprinkling each serving with cilantro.

NOTE The dish can be prepared up to 2 days in advance and refrigerated, tightly covered. Reheat it in a 350°F oven for 20 to 25 minutes, covered, or until hot.

Persian Veal Stew with Rice Pilaf

I adore the use of dried fruits in Persian cooking. Their sweetness balances the aromatic spices in this pilaf so well, and the sprinkling of crunchy nuts adds even more textural interest. The rice, quickly sautéed and then cooked along with everything else, absorbs all the flavors of the dish.

SERVES **4 to 6**

SIZE **6- to 7-quart Dutch oven**

TIME **2 hours**

You will notice that the rice in this dish is first sautéed before it is cooked in liquid. This sauté method "cooks" the starch on the exterior of the grains and keeps them from getting gummy as they cook in the liquid. It also ensures that the cooked rice will be tender at the same time that the veal is properly cooked through.

- 2 **tablespoons unsalted butter**
- ½ **cup slivered blanched almonds**
- 1½ **cups basmati rice**
- 3 **tablespoons olive oil**
- 1½ **pounds boneless veal stew meat, cut into 1½-inch pieces**
- **Salt and freshly ground black pepper, to taste**
- 1 **large onion, diced**
- 2 **large carrots, sliced**
- 3 **garlic cloves, minced**
- 1 **tablespoon grated fresh ginger**
- 1 **teaspoon ground cumin**
- 1 **teaspoon ground coriander**
- ½ **teaspoon ground cardamom**
- 3 **cups Chicken Stock (page 30) or store-bought stock**
- ½ **cup raisins, preferably golden raisins**
- ¼ **cup chopped dried apricots**
- 2 **bay leaves**
- 2 **(3-inch) cinnamon sticks**

Heat the butter in the Dutch oven over medium heat. Add the almonds and cook, stirring constantly, for 1 minute, or until the almonds are brown. Remove the almonds from the pan with a slotted spoon and drain on paper towels. Add the rice to the pan and cook, stirring constantly, for 2 minutes, or until the grains just begin to turn opaque. Remove the rice from the pan and set aside.

Add the oil to the Dutch oven and increase the heat to medium-high. Sprinkle the veal cubes with salt and pepper and brown them in the pan. Remove the veal from the pan with a slotted spoon, and set it aside. Add the onion and carrots to the pan and cook for 2 minutes, stirring frequently. Add the garlic, ginger, cumin, coriander, and cardamom to the pan and cook for 30 seconds, stirring constantly, or until the onion is translucent.

Return the veal to the pan and add the stock, raisins, chopped apricots, bay leaves, and cinnamon sticks. Bring to a boil over medium-high heat, then reduce the heat to low, cover the pan, and cook for 1¼ hours, or until the veal is almost tender. Add the rice to the pan and cook for 20 to 25 minutes, stirring occasionally, or until the veal is tender and the rice has absorbed the liquid.

Remove and discard the bay leaves and cinnamon sticks. Serve immediately, garnishing each serving with some of the almonds.

NOTE The dish can be prepared up to 2 days in advance and refrigerated, tightly covered. Reheat it in a 350°F oven for 20 to 25 minutes, covered, or until hot.

Pot au Feu

Pot au feu, *literally "pot on the fire" in French, is the quintessential winter comfort food, but unlike a steaming bowl of chicken soup, the mélange of meats and vegetables is served in courses. First comes the herbed broth, served with slices of toast on which the marrow from the bones has been spread. Then, accompanied by a few sauces and condiments, the meats are enjoyed. And you'll have a lot of broth left over, so you're all set to make another beefy soup or stew later on.*

SERVES **6 to 8**

SIZE **6- to 7-quart Dutch oven**

TIME **3½ hours**

There are many reasons to add marrow bones to dishes, assuming there's enough room in the pot for them. The first is that the satiny marrow is such a treat to nibble; spread it on toast and sprinkle it with coarse salt. Then, in addition to adding flavor to the broth in which it's cooked, the marrow also adds body, because marrow contains gelatin. The pale white to yellow marrow is soft, fatty tissue from the cavity of large bones where blood cells are produced. It's full of nutrients and it also contains collagen, which helps improve joint function.

1 (2-pound) boneless beef chuck roast
2 pounds veal shanks
5 sprigs fresh parsley
3 sprigs fresh thyme
2 bay leaves
1 head garlic, halved crosswise
2 teaspoons black peppercorns
Salt, to taste
2 to 3 pounds beef marrow bones, cut into 3-inch pieces
3 carrots, cut into 2-inch pieces
1 pound head Savoy cabbage, cut into 8 wedges
4 large Yukon Gold potatoes, halved
4 leeks, white and light green parts, trimmed and halved lengthwise
6 to 8 slices toasted country bread, for serving

SAUCES
½ cup chopped fresh parsley
¼ cup snipped fresh chives
2 tablespoons chopped fresh tarragon
10 cornichons, chopped
¼ cup Dijon mustard
3 tablespoons sherry vinegar
Freshly ground black pepper, to taste
½ cup crème fraîche
3 tablespoons prepared white horseradish

CONDIMENTS
Whole grain mustard
Flaky sea salt

Tie the roast and veal shanks with kitchen string, and place the meats in the Dutch oven. Place the parsley, thyme, bay leaves, garlic, and peppercorns in a triple layer of cheesecloth and tie the bundle tightly to form a bouquet garni. Add the bouquet garni and salt to the Dutch oven and add 3 quarts of water.

Bring the mixture to a boil over high heat. Reduce the heat to low and simmer the mixture, uncovered, for 1¾ hours. Skim the scum that rises to the surface. Add the marrow bones and continue to simmer for another 30 to 45 minutes, or until the meats are tender.

Remove the meats and bones from the broth with tongs, and set them aside to keep warm, covered with aluminum foil. Remove and discard the bouquet garni. If necessary, run a wire-mesh strainer around in the broth to remove any bouquet garni ingredients that may have escaped from the cheesecloth.

Add the carrots, cabbage, and potatoes to the broth and bring to a boil over high heat. Reduce the heat to low and simmer the vegetables, uncovered, for 20 minutes. Add the leeks and simmer for an additional 10 to 15 minutes, or until the vegetables are tender. Remove as much grease as possible from the surface of the broth with a soup ladle.

While the dish cooks, prepare the sauces. Combine the parsley, chives, tarragon, cornichons, mustard, vinegar, and pepper in a small bowl. Stir well. Combine the crème fraîche and horseradish in another small bowl, and stir well. Refrigerate the sauces.

To serve, ladle the broth into bowls, and remove the marrow from the bones with the handle of a wooden spoon. Spread the marrow on the toast slices and serve with the broth.

Carve the meat into slices and pile them on a platter with the vegetables. Allow diners to serve themselves, passing the sauces and bowls of grainy mustard and flaky sea salt separately.

NOTE The dish can be prepared up to 2 days in advance and refrigerated in the Dutch oven.

VARIATION

* **Substitute breast of veal** for the veal shanks and **beef brisket** for the chuck roast.

Beef Stew
with Asian Flavors

It's not just Western cuisines that braise less tender cuts of meat to an ethereal state of fork-tender. Chinese cuisine contains a whole category of what are termed sand-pot stews, named for the earthenware casseroles in which they're cooked. This recipe combines elements of both Chinese and Japanese cooking, with hearty beef and vegetables, many of which are added at the end of the cooking so they remain crisp.

SERVES **4 to 6**

SIZE **6- to 7-quart Dutch oven**

TIME **2¼ hours**

Mirin is a sweet rice wine that is used in countless Japanese recipes for sauces and marinades. It adds mild acidity and has a sweet-tangy flavor. Sweet sherry is a good substitute, or you can also use dry white wine or unseasoned rice wine vinegar with ½ teaspoon of sugar mixed into each tablespoon of wine or vinegar.

1 **bunch scallions, white parts and 6 inches of green tops**
2 **pounds boneless beef chuck, cut into 1½-inch cubes**
Freshly ground black pepper, to taste
2 **tablespoons vegetable oil**
1 **tablespoon toasted sesame oil**
2 **tablespoons minced ginger**
4 **garlic cloves, minced**
1½ **cups Beef Stock (page 29) or store-bought stock**
3 **tablespoons oyster sauce**
3 **tablespoons reduced-sodium soy sauce**
¼ **cup mirin or sweet sherry**

½ **teaspoon Chinese five-spice powder**
½ **lemon**
1½ **pounds sweet potatoes, cut into 1-inch cubes**
2 **parsnips, thickly sliced on the diagonal**
2 **celery ribs, thickly sliced on the diagonal**
1 **red bell pepper, seeds and ribs removed, cut into strips**
2 **tablespoons cornstarch**
½ **pound baby bok choy, thickly sliced on the diagonal**
Salt, to taste

Slice the white parts of the scallions thinly, and slice the green tops into ½-inch pieces on the diagonal. Set them aside separately.

Pat the beef dry with paper towels and sprinkle the cubes with pepper. Heat the vegetable oil and sesame oil in the Dutch oven over medium-high heat. Brown the beef cubes on all sides, turning them gently with tongs. Remove the beef from the pan and set it aside.

Add the scallion whites, ginger, and garlic, and cook for 30 seconds or until fragrant, stirring constantly. Return the beef to the Dutch oven and add the stock, oyster sauce, soy sauce, mirin, five-spice powder, and lemon. Bring to a boil over medium-high heat. Then reduce the heat to low and simmer the beef, covered, for 1¼ hours.

Add the sweet potatoes to the stew, and cook for 30 to 40 minutes, or until the beef is tender. Add the parsnips, celery, and red bell pepper to the stew and cook for 10 minutes, or until the vegetables are crisp-tender. Remove and discard the lemon half.

Combine the cornstarch and 2 tablespoons of cold water in a small cup, and stir the mixture into the stew. Cook over medium heat for 2 minutes, or until slightly thickened. Add the bok choy to the stew and cook for 2 minutes over medium heat. Season with salt and serve immediately, sprinkling each serving with some of the sliced scallion greens.

NOTE The dish can be made up to 2 days in advance and refrigerated, tightly covered. Reheat it over low heat or in a 350°F oven for 30 minutes, or until hot.

VARIATION

* **Substitute cubes of boneless pork butt** for the beef and reduce the initial cooking time to 30 minutes.

Boeuf Bourguignon

This dish from Burgundy, France, is the perfect hearty stew for a fall or winter night. Flavorful from smoky bacon and herbs, the cubes of tender beef and vegetables have a luxurious texture. Of course, serve this dish with a bottle of red wine, preferably one from its native region.

SERVES **4 to 6**

SIZE **6- to 7-quart Dutch oven**

TIME **2½ hours**

Coating food with flour before browning it accomplishes a number of purposes: it creates a brown crust, frying cooks the flour particles, and the finished sauce is lightly thickened from the flour without a lingering "flour-y" taste.

- ⅓ pound thick-sliced bacon, cut into ½-inch-wide strips
- 1 (2-pound) chuck roast, trimmed and cut into 1-inch cubes, or 1½ pounds stewing beef
- Salt and freshly ground black pepper, to taste
- ½ cup all-purpose flour
- 1 large onion, diced
- 3 garlic cloves, minced
- ½ pound small mushrooms, wiped with a damp paper towel, trimmed, and halved, if large
- ¼ cup cognac
- 2 cups dry red wine
- 1 cup Beef Stock (page 29) or store-bought stock
- 2 tablespoons tomato paste
- ¼ cup chopped fresh parsley, divided
- 1 tablespoon fresh thyme leaves
- 1 bay leaf
- 2 carrots, peeled and cut into 1-inch chunks
- 1 pound baby red potatoes, scrubbed, or small red potatoes, quartered

Preheat the oven to 350°F.

Place the Dutch oven over medium-high heat. Cook the bacon for 5 to 7 minutes, or until crisp. Remove the bacon with a slotted spoon, and drain it on paper towels. Set aside. Remove all but 3 tablespoons of the bacon fat from the Dutch oven.

Pat the beef dry with paper towels. Season the beef with salt and pepper, and dust the cubes with flour, shaking off the excess.

Heat the Dutch oven over medium-high heat. Add the beef and cook, turning the pieces with tongs, until brown on all sides. Remove the beef from the pan with a slotted spoon, and set aside.

Add the onion to the pan, and cook, stirring frequently, for 2 minutes. Add the garlic and mushrooms, and cook for 2 more minutes, or until the onion is translucent.

Add the cognac to the pan and cook until it almost evaporates. Add the wine, stock, tomato paste, parsley, thyme, and bay leaf. Stir well, return the meat and bacon to the pan, and bring to a boil on top of the stove, stirring occasionally.

Once it has reached boiling, cover the pan, transfer it to the preheated oven, and bake for 1 hour. Remove the pan from the oven, add the carrots and potatoes, and return the pan to the oven to cook for an additional 1½ hours, or until the meat and potatoes are tender. Remove and discard the bay leaf. Remove as much grease as possible from the surface of the sauce with a soup ladle. Season with salt and serve immediately.

NOTE The dish can be made up to 2 days in advance and refrigerated, tightly covered. Reheat it over low heat or in a 350°F oven for 30 minutes, or until hot.

chapter 4

Saucepans

Saucepans and skillets are the workhorses of the kitchen, and we all have a number of each in various sizes. It's really wasteful to fill a large saucepan with water to boil one egg, and that solitary egg would also look forlorn in a 12-inch skillet.

But all the recipes in this chapter are written for large saucepans because you're cooking a whole meal for four to six people. When we get into the range of 3 to 4 quarts in capacity, there's an alternative to a saucepan that I highly recommend: a saucier, which restaurant chefs have used for generations.

A saucier is essentially a rounded saucepan that has flared walls and curves to the base rather than having a distinct corner at the bottom. It can do everything a saucepan can do, plus it makes some tasks far easier, because foods like polenta and oatmeal don't get lodged in the crease at the base. Sauciers only come as large pots, and they're moderately light when compared to enameled cast iron or stainless steel cookware.

Most good saucepans and sauciers are made with a few different types of metal layered to benefit from the performance strengths of each. Layered cookware is called *clad*; think of those lovely, but *très cher*, All-Clad® pans in specialty kitchen stores. Typically, the outer and inner layer is stainless steel, which is inert and totally nonreactive, but another metal, most typically aluminum or copper, is sandwiched in between—and it conducts heat better than stainless steel.

Another alternative for saucepans, as well as skillets, is anodized aluminum, made famous by Calphalon®. The pan is dark gray, verging on black, and although it has a smooth surface, it isn't coated. Instead, the aluminum is oxidized, which makes it nonporous and nonreactive. One immediate problem, in my book, is that it can't be washed in the dishwasher because strong detergents can harm it, and the anodized surface can break down over time, if you cook a lot of acidic foods that contain ingredients like tomatoes, citrus fruits, or wine sauces.

Enameled cast iron is a good heat conductor, but it's heavy. A 3-quart pan weighs about 10 pounds, whereas a clad pan weighs less than 3 pounds.

Regardless of the weight and metal, make sure that the saucepan has a tight-fitting cover. It's also better to buy one with the handle attached to the outside of the pan without rivets into the interior. The rivets slow down proper cleaning and can leak.

Tuscan Tomato and Bread Stew
(*Pappa al Pomodoro*)

*Nora Pouillon's legendary Restaurant Nora in Washington, DC, ended its 38-year run in June 2017.
Pouillon was an early proponent of organic food and a talented chef. This thick stew is adapted from
the one I enjoyed so often at her restaurant. The soup remains true to its rustic roots (Pouillon didn't
peel tomatoes, nor did she strain away the seeds). It's a straightforward and delicious recipe that's
really quick to make, too. There's bread in the soup, so just serve a tossed salad on the side.*

SERVES **4 to 6**

SIZE **3- to 4-quart saucepan**

TIME **25 minutes**

Don't be stingy with the salt in this dish. There's a large amount of very bland bread serving as the thickening agent, and unless you salt the soup sufficiently, the wonderful ripe tomato flavor won't sing in your mouth.

NOTE The soup can be prepared up to 2 days in advance and refrigerated, tightly covered. Reheat it over low heat, stirring occasionally. Add stock or water if the soup needs thinning after reheating.

VARIATIONS

∗ Add 1 tablespoon **grated orange zest** along with the tomatoes; substitute **crushed red pepper flakes** for the black pepper.

¼ cup extra-virgin olive oil
3 garlic cloves, minced
2 pounds ripe tomatoes, cored and coarsely chopped
4 cups Vegetable Stock (page 33), Chicken Stock (page 30), or store-bought stock

5 cups firmly packed day-old country bread, diced
½ cup firmly packed fresh sliced basil
Salt and freshly ground black pepper, to taste
Freshly grated Parmesan cheese, for serving

Heat the oil in the saucepan over medium-low heat. Add the garlic and cook, stirring frequently, for 30 to 45 seconds, or until the garlic begins to brown. Add the tomatoes and stock and cook over medium-high heat, stirring occasionally, for 15 minutes, or until the tomatoes break down.

Stir the bread cubes into the soup and cook over medium-low heat, uncovered and stirring occasionally, for 10 minutes, or until the bread falls apart.

Stir in the basil and season with salt and pepper. Serve immediately, passing around the Parmesan separately at the table.

Indonesian Vegetarian Pasta with Peanut Sauce

This pasta dish, cooked in one pan, draws its inspiration from the peanut noodles of Indonesia. The vegetables remain crisp, and the dish can be served cold or hot. It is also open to almost endless variation.

SERVES **4 to 6**

SIZE **3- to 4-quart saucepan**

TIME **15 minutes**

Hoisin sauce, pronounced *hoy-ZAHN*, is a complexly flavored Asian ingredient and condiment made from soybeans, sugar, vinegar, garlic, and chiles. It adds spicy, salty, and sweet elements to recipes and is also used as a condiment. Hoisin sauce is spread onto Mandarin pancakes when rolling up mu shu pork or Peking duck, and it's also used as a dipping sauce for appetizers.

12 ounces dry spaghetti or linguine
4 cups Vegetable Stock (page 33) or store-bought stock
¼ cup commercial peanut butter
2 tablespoons tomato paste
2 tablespoons soy sauce
2 tablespoons hoisin sauce
2 tablespoons unseasoned rice wine vinegar
3 garlic cloves, minced
2 tablespoons minced fresh ginger
½ teaspoon crushed red pepper flakes, or to taste
1 large carrot, thinly sliced
1 red bell pepper, seeds and ribs removed, thinly sliced

2 cups firmly packed fresh bok choy
2 tablespoons freshly squeezed lime juice
4 scallions, white parts and 4 inches of green tops, thinly sliced
Salt and freshly ground black pepper, to taste
½ cup chopped salted peanuts, for serving
¼ cup chopped fresh cilantro, for serving

Break the pasta into 1½-inch pieces, and set it aside. Combine the stock, peanut butter, tomato paste, soy sauce, hoisin sauce, vinegar, garlic, ginger, and crushed red pepper in the saucepan, and whisk well to dissolve the tomato paste and peanut butter.

Bring the mixture to a boil over high heat. Add the pasta, reduce the heat to medium-low, cover the pan, and simmer the mixture for 4 minutes. Add the carrot and red bell pepper and cook for 4 to 6 minutes, stirring every few minutes. Uncover the pan, add the bok choy, and cook for 2 to 3 minutes, or until the bok choy is crisp-tender.

Stir in the lime juice and scallions, and season with salt and pepper. Serve immediately, garnishing each serving with chopped peanuts and cilantro.

NOTE Before adding the scallions and lime juice, the dish can be cooked up to 2 days in advance and refrigerated, tightly covered. Reheat it over low heat, covered, before completing the dish, or serve it cold.

VARIATIONS

∗ **Substitute chicken stock** for the vegetable stock and add 1 pound of thinly sliced boneless skinless chicken breasts or thighs to the dish with the pasta, carrot, and bell pepper.

∗ **Substitute seafood stock** for the vegetable stock and add 1 pound of peeled and deveined shrimp to the dish along with the bok choy.

Mac and Cheese
with Tomatoes and Herbs

This dish represents the marriage of pasta in a creamy tomato sauce and mac and cheese. Kids love it because it's mac and cheese, and adults appreciate the subtle seasoning and burst of flavor provided by the Gorgonzola. Serve it with a tossed salad.

SERVES **Serves 4 to 6**

SIZE **3- to 4-quart saucepan**

TIME **12 minutes**

Sporting a network of blue veins, Gorgonzola is one of the named products of Lombardy and Piedmont. It is made from cow's milk. While we're accustomed to Gorgonzola naturale, after World War II Gorgonzola dolce (meaning sweet) joined its ranks. It's a milder version that is neither cooked nor pressed, and it's aged for about half the time as its more assertive prototype.

NOTE The dish can be prepared up to 2 days in advance and refrigerated, tightly covered. Reheat it over low heat, covered, stirring occasionally. Add milk or cream if the dish needs thinning after reheating.

2 tablespoons unsalted butter
2 shallots, diced
2 garlic cloves, minced
¼ cup dry white wine
2 tablespoons tomato paste
2 cups whole milk
1 cup light cream
1 (14½-ounce) can petite diced tomatoes, undrained
¼ cup chopped fresh basil
2 tablespoons chopped fresh oregano
¾ pound elbow macaroni
4 ounces whole-milk mozzarella, grated
2 ounces Gorgonzola, crumbled
Salt and freshly ground black pepper, to taste

Heat the butter in the saucepan over medium heat. Add the shallots and cook, stirring frequently, for 2 minutes. Add the garlic and cook for 1 minute, or until the shallots are translucent. Add the wine, increase the heat to medium-high, and cook for 2 minutes, or until the wine has almost evaporated.

Stir in the tomato paste, milk, cream, tomatoes, basil, oregano, and macaroni. Bring to a boil over medium heat, stirring frequently to keep the macaroni from clumping. Cook the mixture for 4 to 5 minutes, stirring occasionally, or until the pasta is tender.

Remove the pan from the stove and stir in the mozzarella and Gorgonzola. Season with salt and pepper, and serve immediately.

Curried Fish Stew

The curry and chile are tamed by creamy coconut milk and rich peanut butter in this Indian-inspired fish stew. Adding some vegetables at the end of the cooking process enlivens the texture, too.

SERVES **4 to 6**

SIZE **3- to 4-quart saucepan**

TIME **20 minutes**

2 tablespoons vegetable oil

1 small onion, chopped

2 jalapeño or serrano chiles, seeds and ribs removed, chopped

4 garlic cloves, minced

3 tablespoons curry powder

½ teaspoon ground cinnamon
Pinch of ground allspice

½ cup Seafood Stock (page 32) or store-bought stock

3 tablespoons natural peanut butter

1 (15-ounce) can light coconut milk

1 teaspoon granulated sugar

1 pound redskin potatoes, scrubbed and cut into ¾-inch dice

2 carrots, peeled and sliced

1¼ pounds thick white firm-fleshed fish fillets, such as halibut or cod, cut into 1-inch cubes

2 ounces fresh snow peas or sugar-snap peas, stemmed

Salt and freshly ground black pepper, to taste

¼ cup chopped fresh cilantro, for serving

Heat the oil in the saucepan over medium-high heat. Add the onion and chiles, and cook, stirring frequently, for 3 minutes, or until the onion is translucent. Add the garlic, curry powder, cinnamon, and allspice, and cook for 1 minute, stirring constantly. Scrape the mixture into a food processor fitted with the steel blade or into a blender. Add the stock and peanut butter, and puree until smooth.

Return the puree to the saucepan, and add the coconut milk and sugar. Bring to a boil over medium-high heat, stirring occasionally. Add the potatoes and carrots, and bring to a boil. Reduce the heat to low, cover the pan, and simmer for 12 to 15 minutes, or until the vegetables are tender.

Add the fish to the pan, and cook for 2 minutes. Add the snow peas and cook for an additional 1½ minutes, or until the fish is cooked through and flakes easily. Season with salt and pepper, and serve immediately, sprinkling each serving with cilantro.

While I'm no fan of skim milk or even 2% milk, I always look for the light version of canned coconut milk. Just ¼ cup of coconut milk runs about 140 calories, while the light version is 40 calories for the same size serving. And for cooking, you must use the canned product. The refrigerated coconut milk next to the nut milks in the refrigerator case does not really deliver any coconut flavor.

NOTE The dish can be prepared up to 1 day in advance and refrigerated, tightly covered. Reheat it over low heat, covered, until hot, stirring occasionally.

VARIATION

* **Substitute chicken stock** for the seafood stock, and substitute 1¼ pounds boneless, skinless chicken breast, cut into 1-inch cubes, for the fish. Add the chicken to the stew along with the potatoes and carrots.

Bahamian Fish Stew

The islands of the Caribbean have produced many delicious fish soups and stews, including this one. It's spiked with rum and allspice to add a tropical twist. Serve it over rice with some cornbread alongside.

SERVES **4 to 6**

SIZE **3- to 4-quart saucepan**

TIME **25 minutes**

Allspice got its name because its flavor and aroma are reminiscent of a combination of spices—cinnamon, nutmeg, and cloves. If you don't have allspice around, use a pinch of those spices to replicate the flavor.

NOTE The stew can be prepared up to 1 day in advance and refrigerated, tightly covered. Reheat it over low heat, covered, until hot, stirring occasionally.

VARIATION

* **Substitute chicken stock** for the seafood stock, and substitute 1¼ pounds boneless, skinless chicken breasts, cut into 1-inch cubes, for the fish. Add the chicken to the stew after the vegetables have cooked for 5 minutes.

3 tablespoons olive oil
1 large onion, diced
1 red bell pepper, seeds and ribs removed, diced
2 carrots, diced
2 celery ribs, diced
3 garlic cloves, minced
6 cups Seafood Stock (page 32) or store-bought stock
2 tablespoons tomato paste
2 tablespoons Worcestershire sauce
2 tablespoons rum, preferably dark rum
3 tablespoons chopped fresh cilantro
2 teaspoons fresh thyme leaves
¼ teaspoon ground allspice
½ teaspoon hot red pepper sauce, or to taste
1 bay leaf
1 pound sweet potatoes, peeled and cut into ¾-inch dice
1 cup cherry or grape tomatoes, halved
1¼ pounds thick white firm-fleshed fish fillets, such as cod or halibut, cut into 1-inch cubes
Salt and freshly ground black pepper, to taste

Heat oil in the saucepan over medium-high heat. Add the onion, red bell pepper, carrots, and celery. Cook, stirring frequently, for 2 minutes. Add the garlic and cook for 1 minute, or until the onion is translucent.

Add the stock and tomato paste, and stir well to dissolve tomato paste. Add the Worcestershire sauce, rum, cilantro, thyme, allspice, hot red pepper sauce, bay leaf, and sweet potatoes. Bring to a boil, stirring occasionally.

Reduce the heat to low, and simmer the stew, partially covered, for 15 to 20 minutes, or until the vegetables are tender. Add the cherry tomatoes and fish, cover the pan again, and cook for 3 to 5 minutes, or until the fish is cooked and flakes easily. Remove and discard the bay leaf, season with salt and pepper, and serve immediately.

Jambalaya Salad

Jambalaya is native to the Louisiana bayous, and many experts believe that the name comes from the Spanish word for ham, jamón. *This cold salad has the same vivid flavors as the dish when it is served hot. I love it with a dry rosé or a glass of beer.*

SERVES **4 to 6**

SIZE **3- to 4-quart saucepan**

COOKING TIME **25 minutes**   CHILLING TIME **Minimum of 2 hours**

In restaurant kitchens there's usually a rack for sheet pans in the walk-in refrigerator, because spreading hot food in a thin layer onto a cold surface is the fastest way to chill it. If your refrigerator doesn't have space to hold a large pan, divide the hot cooked rice and meats onto two or three dinner plates so that the mixture is only a few inches deep. Chill the plates individually, and the dish will be ready to serve in less than an hour.

SALAD

- 3 tablespoons olive oil
- 1 medium onion, chopped
- 1 celery rib, chopped
- 1 jalapeño or serrano chile, seeds and ribs removed, chopped
- ½ green bell pepper, seeds and ribs removed, chopped
- 1 cup long-grain white rice
- 2 garlic cloves, minced
- 2 cups tomato juice
- 2 tablespoons chopped fresh parsley
- 2 teaspoons fresh thyme leaves
- 1 bay leaf
- ½ pound boneless, skinless chicken breast, cut into 1-inch cubes
- ½ pound large (16 to 20 per pound) raw shrimp, peeled, deveined, and cut in half lengthwise
- ¼ pound baked ham, cut into ½-inch dice
- 6 scallions, white parts and 4 inches of green tops, thinly sliced
- ½ yellow or orange bell pepper, seeds and ribs removed, diced
- ½ cup cooked green peas, for serving

DRESSING

- ¼ cup freshly squeezed lemon juice
- 3 garlic cloves, minced
- 1 teaspoon dried oregano
- Salt, to taste
- Hot red pepper sauce, to taste
- ½ cup olive oil

Heat the olive oil in the saucepan over medium-high heat. Add the onion, celery, jalapeño, and green pepper. Cook, stirring frequently, for 3 minutes, or until the onion is translucent. Add the rice and garlic, and cook for 2 minutes, stirring constantly.

(continued on the following page)

(continued from the previous page)

Add the tomato juice, parsley, thyme, and bay leaf. Bring to a boil over medium-high heat, and then reduce the heat to low and simmer, covered, for 10 minutes. Add the chicken cubes, bring the mixture back to a boil, and simmer for 5 minutes. Add the shrimp, and cook for an additional 5 minutes, or until the chicken is cooked through and no longer pink, and the rice is tender. Remove and discard the bay leaf.

Spread the mixture onto a sheet pan or several plates and chill it well. Transfer the rice mixture to a serving bowl and fold in the ham, scallions, and bell pepper.

To make the dressing, combine the lemon juice, garlic, oregano, salt, and hot red pepper sauce in a jar with a tight-fitting lid and shake well. Add the oil, and shake well again.

Toss half of the dressing with the salad to moisten it. Serve immediately, garnishing the salad with peas. Pass the remaining dressing separately.

NOTE The salad and dressing can be prepared 1 day in advance and refrigerated, tightly covered. Do not toss the salad with the dressing until ready to serve.

Spicy Israeli Couscous with Chicken and Baby Spinach

These large pasta beads, also called pearl couscous, *have become really popular over the past few years. They take on a nutty flavor if they're toasted before cooking. In this easy-to-make recipe, the spicy flavor comes from a combination of ginger, red pepper, and harissa, but then it's softened, at the end, with aromatic tahini. Serve the couscous with a tossed salad.*

SERVES **4 to 6**

SIZE **3- to 4-quart saucepan**

TIME **15 minutes**

Harissa is one of my favorite condiments, and I use it to brighten up flavors even in dishes that don't have North African roots. Add a tablespoon or two to chopped meat when making burgers, or to spice up a bowl of hummus. I also like to add it to both vinegar and mayonnaise-based dressings.

1½ pounds boneless, skinless chicken breasts
¼ cup olive oil, divided
1½ cups (6 ounces) Israeli couscous
1 small onion, diced
2 tablespoons minced fresh ginger
2 garlic cloves, minced
2 teaspoons ground cumin
½ teaspoon crushed red pepper flakes
1 to 2 tablespoons harissa paste

1 tablespoon chopped fresh rosemary
2½ cups Chicken Stock (page 30) or store-bought stock
¼ pound baby spinach
2 to 3 tablespoons well-stirred tahini
Salt and freshly ground black pepper, to taste

Pat the chicken dry with paper towels, and slice it against the grain into ½-inch thick slices. Set aside.

Heat 2 tablespoons of the olive oil in the saucepan over medium-high heat. Add the couscous and cook, stirring frequently, until the grains are brown. Remove the couscous from the pan.

Heat the remaining oil in the saucepan over medium-high heat. Add the onion and ginger and cook, stirring frequently, for 2 minutes. Add the garlic, cumin, crushed red pepper flakes, harissa, and rosemary. Cook for 1 minute, stirring constantly. Add the chicken slices and stir to coat them evenly.

Return the couscous to the saucepan and add the stock. Bring to a boil, reduce the heat to low, cover the pan, and cook for 10 to 12 minutes, or until the liquid has almost been absorbed and the chicken is cooked through and no longer pink.

Add the spinach by handfuls, allowing the leaves to wilt before adding more. Stir in the tahini, season with salt and pepper, and serve immediately.

NOTE The dish can be prepared up to 2 days in advance and refrigerated, tightly covered. Reheat it over low heat, adding more stock while reheating it if it seems dry.

Creamy Mexican Chicken and Corn Chowder

Chipotle chiles (smoked jalapeño chiles) add a smoky dimension to this creamy corn-flecked chowder. Warm corn tortillas and a salad with avocado work well to complete the meal.

SERVES **4 to 6**

SIZE **3- to 4-quart saucepan**

TIME **30 minutes**

Canned cream-style corn doesn't contain any dairy products. Its creamy texture is the result of grinding up some kernels, which allows the natural starch to come out. As is the case with most canned vegetable products, whenever possible purchase cans that do not have any additional salt added.

NOTE The soup can be prepared up to 2 days in advance and refrigerated, tightly covered. Reheat it over low heat, covered, until hot, stirring occasionally.

VARIATION

* **Substitute 1 (4-ounce) can chopped mild green chiles**, drained, for the chipotle chiles and adobo sauce for a less spicy soup.

- 3 tablespoons unsalted butter
- 1¼ pounds boneless, skinless chicken thighs, cut into 1-inch cubes
- ½ red bell pepper, seeds and ribs removed, diced
- ½ yellow bell pepper, seeds and ribs removed, diced
- 1 large onion, diced
- 2 garlic cloves, minced
- 2 teaspoons ground cumin
- ½ teaspoon dried oregano, preferably Mexican oregano
- 2 medium sweet potatoes, peeled and cut into ¾-inch dice
- 2½ cups Chicken Stock (page 30) or store-bought stock
- 2 canned chipotle chiles in adobo sauce, finely chopped
- 1 tablespoon adobo sauce
- 1 (15-ounce) can cream-style corn
- 1 cup fresh corn kernels (from 2 ears), or substitute frozen kernels
- 2 cups half-and-half or whole milk
  Salt and freshly ground black pepper, to taste
- 3 tablespoons chopped fresh cilantro, for serving (optional)

Heat the butter in a saucepan over medium-high heat. Add the chicken, and cook for 2 minutes, or until the chicken is opaque. Add the red and yellow bell peppers and onion. Cook, stirring frequently, for 2 minutes. Add the garlic, cumin, and oregano. Cook, stirring constantly, for 1 minute, or until the onion is translucent. Add the sweet potatoes, stock, chipotle chiles, and adobo sauce to the saucepan, and stir well.

Bring to a boil over medium-high heat, then reduce the heat to low and simmer the soup, covered, for 20 minutes. Add the creamed corn, corn kernels, and half-and-half, and simmer for 5 minutes, or until the chicken is cooked through and no longer pink, and the vegetables are tender. Season with salt and pepper, and serve immediately, sprinkling each serving with cilantro, if desired.

Chicken Chili
with Tomatillos

*Tomatillos are more closely related to gooseberries than to tomatoes,
and they have a tangy flavor with light citrus notes. They form the base
of this easy salsa verde, in which chicken and vegetables are cooked.*

SERVES **4 to 6**

SIZE **3- to 4-quart saucepan**

TIME **45 minutes**

The real heat in chiles is found in the seeds and the ribs, so you can always adjust a dish to your liking by either removing the seeds and ribs or leaving them in. When you see a recipe calling for more than one chile pepper, it's likely that the seeds are meant to be discarded.

1 **pound tomatillos, husked and rinsed**
2 **or 3 jalapeño or serrano chiles, seeds and ribs removed, diced**
1 **shallot, sliced**
½ **cup firmly packed fresh cilantro leaves**
2 **tablespoons olive oil**
1 **large onion, diced**
1 **red bell pepper, seeds and ribs removed, diced**
3 **garlic cloves, minced**
1 **tablespoon ground cumin**
1½ **pounds boneless, skinless chicken thighs**
2 **large sweet potatoes, cut into 1-inch cubes**

2 **cups Chicken Stock (page 30) or store-bought stock**
Salt **and freshly ground black pepper, to taste**
2 **small yellow summer squash, halved lengthwise and cut into ¾-inch slices**
1 **(15-ounce) can kidney beans, drained and rinsed**
1 **(15-ounce) can garbanzo beans, drained and rinsed**
1 **diced avocado, for serving**
½ **cup sour cream, for serving**
¼ **cup chopped fresh cilantro, for serving**
3 **scallions, white parts and 4 inches of green tops, sliced, for serving**

Place the tomatillos in the saucepan and cover them with water. Bring to a boil over high heat, then reduce the heat to low and simmer the tomatillos for 6 to 8 minutes, or until they turn from bright green to olive green. Drain the tomatillos and dice them when cool enough to handle.

(continued on the following page)

(continued from the previous page)

Combine the tomatillos, chiles, shallot, and cilantro in a food processor fitted with a steel blade or in a blender. Puree, and scrape the mixture into a bowl.

Heat the oil in the saucepan over medium-high heat. Add the onion and red bell pepper and cook, stirring frequently, for 2 minutes. Add the garlic and cumin and cook for 1 minute, stirring constantly, or until the onion is translucent.

Add the tomatillo puree to the saucepan along with the chicken, sweet potatoes, and stock. Season with salt and pepper and simmer over low heat, covered, for 30 minutes. Add the summer squash and beans and cook for an additional 10 to 12 minutes, or until the sweet potatoes and squash are tender.

Remove the chicken thighs from the pan with tongs, and shred the meat with two forks. Return the meat to the pan and adjust the seasoning as needed. Serve in low bowls, passing around dishes containing avocado, sour cream, cilantro, and scallions as garnishes.

NOTE The dish can be prepared up to 2 days in advance and refrigerated, tightly covered. Reheat it, covered, over low heat.

VARIATION

* **Substitute 1½ pounds peeled and deveined shrimp** for the chicken and **substitute seafood stock** for the chicken stock. Add the shrimp to the dish along with the summer squash and beans.

Moroccan Chicken Salad with Dried Fruit and Olives

Tangy dried currants and succulent dried apricots meld with traditional Moroccan spices and add textural interest to the light couscous base of this aromatic chicken salad. It's refreshing on a summer day.

SERVES **4 to 6**

SIZE **3- to 4-quart saucepan**

COOKING TIME **25 minutes** · CHILLING TIME **Minimum of 2 hours**

While arugula may resemble spinach, it's more closely related to watercress and dandelion greens. It has a peppery kick, which makes it a real flavor player in salads, rather than just offering a bit of cool and crunchy texture.

SALAD

- 3 tablespoons olive oil
- 2 cups Israeli couscous
- 2 cups Chicken Stock (page 30) or store-bought stock
- ½ cup freshly squeezed orange juice
- 1 tablespoon harissa
- ⅓ cup dried currants
- ⅓ cup chopped dried apricots
- Salt and freshly ground black pepper, to taste
- 1 pound boneless, skinless chicken breast, cut into 1-inch cubes
- 1 (15-ounce) can garbanzo beans, drained and rinsed
- ½ cup pitted and chopped Kalamata olives
- ½ small red onion, diced
- ½ small fennel bulb, trimmed and diced
- 3 ounces (3 cups) baby arugula, roughly chopped
- ½ cup shelled and chopped pistachio nuts, for serving

DRESSING

- ¼ cup freshly squeezed orange juice
- 2 tablespoons balsamic vinegar
- ¼ cup chopped fresh cilantro
- 4 garlic cloves, minced
- 1 tablespoon ground cumin
- 1 teaspoon grated orange zest
- Salt and freshly ground black pepper, to taste
- ⅓ cup olive oil

Heat the oil in the pan over medium heat. Add the couscous and cook, stirring frequently, for 4 to 5 minutes, or until about half of it is lightly browned. Add the stock, orange juice, harissa, currants, and apricots, and season with salt and pepper. Bring to a boil, reduce the heat to low, and cook covered for 4 minutes. Stir in the chicken, and cook for an additional 8 minutes, stirring occasionally, or until the liquid is absorbed and the chicken is cooked through and no longer pink. Allow the couscous to rest, covered, for 3 minutes.

Spread the mixture onto a sheet pan or several dinner plates and chill it well for at least 2 hours.

Transfer the couscous mixture to a serving bowl and fold in the garbanzo beans, olives, red onion, fennel, and arugula.

For the dressing, combine the orange juice, vinegar, cilantro, garlic, cumin, orange zest, salt, and pepper in a jar with a tight-fitting lid. Shake well. Add the olive oil and shake well again. Set aside.

Toss half of the dressing with the salad to moisten it. Serve immediately, garnishing the salad with the pistachio nuts. Pass around the remaining dressing.

NOTE The salad and dressing can be prepared 1 day in advance and refrigerated, tightly covered. Do not toss the salad with the dressing until ready to serve.

VARIATION

* **Substitute seafood stock** for the chicken stock and **peeled and deveined shrimp** for the chicken. Cook the couscous for 8 minutes before adding the shrimp to the dish.

Summer Corn Chowder

In the summertime, I'll pass up even homegrown tomatoes for ears of fresh summer corn. I'm fondest of the bicolor "sugar and butter" variety that's harvested in New England—and it's featured in a few recipes in this book. A bowl of chowder, like this one, is fantastic served with some crusty bread. Corn is definitely the star, and the leeks and carrots accentuate its innate sweetness.

SERVES **4 to 6**

SIZE **3- to 4-quart saucepan**

TIME **25 minutes**

Once an ear of corn is harvested, the natural sugars immediately begin to turn to starch, which is why it's best to buy corn from a roadside farm stand whenever possible. The sweetness of an ear of corn is also determined by the way it is cooked. Bring a large pan of salted water to a boil over high heat. Add the corn and cover the pan. As soon as the water returns to a boil, turn off the heat and allow the corn to sit, covered, for 5 minutes before eating it. The benefit of this method is that the corn can sit in the water for up to a few hours and it won't overcook.

6 to 8 ears fresh corn, shucked, with silk removed
¼ pound thick-sliced bacon
1 large leek, white and pale green part, sliced
1 medium carrot, diced
2 celery ribs, diced
3 Yukon Gold potatoes, peeled and cut into ½-inch dice
3 cups Chicken Stock (page 30) or store-bought stock
1 tablespoon fresh thyme leaves
1 bay leaf
2 cups half-and-half
¼ pound fresh green beans, cut into 1-inch pieces
Salt and freshly ground black pepper, to taste

Cut the kernels off the corncobs, reserving the cobs. Set aside the kernels and break or cut the cobs in half.

Heat a saucepan over medium-high heat. Cook the bacon in the pan for 5 to 7 minutes, or until crisp. Remove the bacon from the pan with a slotted spoon and drain on paper towels. Set aside.

Discard all but 2 tablespoons of the bacon grease from the pan. Add the leek, carrot, and celery, and cook for 3 minutes, stirring occasionally, or until the leek is translucent. Add the reserved corncobs, potatoes, stock, thyme, and bay leaf. Bring to a boil over medium-high heat. Reduce the heat to low and simmer the soup, uncovered, for 10 minutes, or until the vegetables are almost tender.

While the soup simmers, puree half of the corn kernels with the half-and-half in a food processor fitted with a steel blade or in a blender.

Remove the corncobs from the pan with tongs and transfer them to a colander. Place the colander over the saucepan and press the corncobs with the back of a spoon to extract as much liquid as possible. Discard the corncobs.

Return the bacon to the pan and add the corn kernels, corn puree, and green beans. Bring the mixture to a boil over medium heat, then reduce the heat to low and simmer the chowder for 2 to 3 minutes, or until the green beans are crisp-tender. Remove and discard the bay leaf, season with salt and pepper, and serve hot.

NOTE The soup can be prepared up to 2 days in advance and refrigerated, tightly covered. Reheat it over low heat, stirring occasionally. Add milk or cream if the soup needs thinning after reheating.

Turkey Chili Blanca

Blanca means "white" in Spanish, and that's the color of this thick and flavorful tomato-free stew, made with ground turkey and white beans, and thickened with barley. Serve it with a tossed salad.

SERVES **4 to 6**

SIZE **3- to 4-quart saucepan**

TIME **50 to 55 minutes**

The process that differentiates hulled barley from pearl barley is similar to the one that determines whether rice is marketed as brown or white. While all barley must have its fibrous outer hull removed before it can be eaten, pearl barley is then polished to remove the bran layer as well. Hulled barley takes almost twice as long to cook, so the two types of barley cannot be substituted for one another.

NOTE The dish can be prepared up to 2 days in advance and refrigerated, tightly covered. Reheat it, covered, over low heat, stirring occasionally, until hot.

VARIATION

∗ **Substitute ground beef** for the ground turkey and **substitute beef stock** for the chicken stock.

2 tablespoons olive oil
1 medium onion, diced
½ green bell pepper, seeds and ribs removed, chopped
1 large jalapeño or serrano chile, seeds and ribs removed, finely chopped
4 garlic cloves, minced
1 pound ground turkey
1½ tablespoons ground cumin
1½ teaspoons dried oregano, preferably Mexican
3 cups Chicken Stock (page 30) or store-bought stock
⅓ cup pearl barley
2 (15-ounce) cans cannellini beans, drained and rinsed
¼ cup chopped fresh cilantro
Salt, to taste
Hot red pepper sauce, to taste
4 scallions, white parts and 4 inches of green tops, sliced, for serving
¾ cup grated Monterey Jack cheese, for serving
½ cup sour cream, for serving

Heat the oil in the saucepan over medium-high heat. Add the onion, green bell pepper, and chile. Cook, stirring frequently, for 2 minutes. Add the garlic and cook for 1 minute, or until the onion is translucent. Add the turkey, breaking up lumps with a fork, and cook for 3 minutes. Add the cumin and oregano, and cook for 1 minute, stirring constantly.

Add the stock and barley, and bring to a boil over medium-high heat. Reduce the heat to low, cover the pan, and simmer the chili for 30 minutes, stirring occasionally.

Add the beans and cilantro, and simmer the chili, uncovered, stirring occasionally, for 15 to 20 minutes, or until the barley is tender. Season with salt and hot red pepper sauce, and serve immediately, passing the scallions, cheese, and sour cream separately.

Mac and Cheese with Country Ham and Spinach

This mac and cheese is lighter than most because the pasta is braised in stock before the cream, cheeses, herbs, spinach, and country ham are added. I usually serve this dish with a bowl of crunchy coleslaw on the side.

SERVES 4 to 6

SIZE 3- to 4-quart quart saucepan

TIME 18 minutes

Country ham is becoming easier to find in most stores around the country, but you can always substitute Italian prosciutto or Spanish serrano ham to deliver the satiny texture and salty flavor of this uncooked salt-cured ham.

NOTE The dish can be prepared up to 2 days in advance and refrigerated, tightly covered. Reheat it over low heat, covered, stirring occasionally. Add milk or cream if the dish needs thinning after reheating.

VARIATION

∗ For a vegetarian dish, omit the ham and **substitute smoked Gouda** for the aged Gouda to deliver a similar flavor.

2 tablespoons vegetable oil
¾ pound macaroni
3 cups Chicken Stock (page 30) or store-bought stock, divided
⅔ cup heavy cream
¼ pound aged Gouda, grated
1½ ounces freshly grated Parmesan cheese
¼ pound baby spinach
¼ pound country ham, cut into fine julienne
1 tablespoon chopped fresh parsley
2 teaspoons chopped fresh rosemary
Salt and freshly ground black pepper, to taste

Heat the vegetable oil in the saucepan over medium heat. Add half the pasta and cook, stirring frequently, for 3 minutes, or until golden brown. Add the remaining pasta and 1½ cups of the stock. Cook for 5 minutes, or until most of the stock is absorbed. Add the remaining stock and cook, stirring frequently, for 5 to 6 minutes, or until all of the stock is absorbed.

Stir in the cream and Gouda and Parmesan cheeses. Cook over low heat until the cheeses melt. Add the spinach, ham, parsley, and rosemary and cook for 1½ to 2 minutes, or until the spinach wilts. Season with salt and pepper and serve immediately.

Cuban Picadillo

Picadillo, pronounced peek-ah-DEE-oh, *is a first cousin to Tex-Mex chili con carne, but it has a more interesting flavor profile because of the addition of the salty olives and capers, and sweet raisins. Picadillo is the quintessential comfort food, and, because it includes potatoes, no other carbohydrate is necessary to complete the meal.*

SERVES **4 to 6**

SIZE **3- to 4-quart saucepan**

TIME **1 hour**

Here's an easy way to remove the seeds and ribs from bell peppers: Cut a slice off the bottom so the pepper stands up straight. You'll see that there are natural curves to the sections. Holding the pepper by its stem, cut down those curves, and you'll be left with a skeleton of ribs and seeds. Throw it out, and you're ready to chop the pepper.

2 tablespoons olive oil
2 medium onions, diced
1 red bell pepper, seeds and ribs removed, diced
3 garlic cloves, minced
1 tablespoon ground cumin
2 teaspoons ground cinnamon
2 teaspoons dried oregano, preferably Mexican
Pinch of freshly grated nutmeg
1¼ pounds lean ground beef
½ cup dry sherry
1 (28-ounce) can whole tomatoes, drained and crushed

½ cup sliced green olives
2 tablespoons olive brine
½ cup raisins
2 bay leaves
2 large Yukon Gold potatoes, peeled and cut into ½-inch dice
2 tablespoons capers, drained and rinsed
1 (15-ounce) can red kidney beans, drained and rinsed
Salt and freshly ground black pepper, to taste
⅓ cup chopped fresh cilantro, for serving

Heat the oil in the saucepan over medium-high heat. Add the onions and red bell pepper and cook, stirring frequently, for 2 minutes. Add the garlic, cumin, cinnamon, oregano, and nutmeg and cook for 1 minute, stirring constantly, or until the onions are translucent.

Crumble the beef into the pan and cook, breaking up lumps with a fork, for 4 minutes, or until the beef loses its red color. Add the sherry and cook over high heat for 3 minutes, or until it has almost evaporated. Add the tomatoes, olives, olive brine, raisins, bay leaves, and potatoes. Bring to a boil, reduce the heat to low, and let the dish simmer, covered, for 30 minutes. Uncover the pan, stir in the capers and beans, and cook for another 10 minutes. Season with salt and pepper, remove and discard the bay leaves, and serve immediately, sprinkling each serving with cilantro.

NOTE The dish can be made up to 2 days in advance and refrigerated, tightly covered. Reheat it, covered, over low heat until it simmers.

chapter 5

Skillets

While in some chapters of this book all you need is one pan to successfully complete the recipes, in this one, when it comes to skillets, you really need a few. Not only do you need at least two skillet sizes—a 10-inch and a 12-inch—you'll also need one skillet made of cast iron and another of clad stainless steel.

Skillets are frying pans with low, flared sides that encourage evaporation. This makes them the perfect shape for searing food, browning it well, and reducing sauces. You can shallow fry in a skillet, and you can also stir-fry in one. And the base is wide enough that you can cook a lot of food at the same time.

I'm devoted to cast iron. After all, I'm the author of *The New Cast Iron Skillet Cookbook*, which was published by Sterling in 2014. But cast iron is heavy, and it needs special attention, both before its first use and after cooking with it. That's why I also love skillets that are "clad"—pans that have an aluminum core, an excellent conductor of heat, sandwiched between two layers of stainless steel. Not only do these skillets cook well, they can be washed in the dishwasher.

There are health benefits associated with cooking food in cast iron. Dietary iron is an important nutrient that we need on a daily basis to maintain high energy levels and support the immune system, and some of this mineral leaches into food that is cooked in a cast iron skillet. The amount of iron varies, depending on the type of food being cooked, the acidity level of the food, and the length of time the food remains in contact with the skillet.

Clad skillets are more expensive than cast iron, but there is a workaround. Some skillets have just a clad bottom and stainless steel sides. And one way to avoid the tender care needed to preserve the seasoning of a cast iron skillet is to buy one that has a coating of enamel over the iron. An enameled cast iron skillet is not as forgiving as a clad pan; you can't use it under the broiler or on the grill, but it can definitely go into the dishwasher.

A few of the recipes specify an ovenproof skillet. That means that the handle is metal and not covered by heatproof plastic. If all you have are skillets with plastic handles, one way to make them ovenproof is to wrap the handle in a few layers of aluminum foil.

You'll notice that I'm ignoring any conversation of nonstick skillets sold at a variety of price levels. That's because I really do fear the chemicals in the coating, and the coating inevitably chips off and can leach into the food. If the chemical fumes can kill someone's pet canary, I don't want them in my house.

Seasoning a Cast Iron Skillet

The beauty of cast iron is that it provides a non-stick surface that's as smooth as glass without any chemicals. If you buy a skillet that's seasoned by the manufacturer, just start cooking. But if you find a wonderful antique skillet at a yard sale or inherit one from an aunt, chances are you'll need to give it some TLC.

I use the method first published by food blogger Sheryl Canter. While cast iron skillets go back more than a millennium, Canter's method is truly twenty-first century and uses an oil I'd never seen referenced in regard to cast iron cookery—flaxseed oil. Flaxseed oil is not shelved in the supermarket with the olive oil. It's sold as a dietary supplement because of its high content of omega-3 fatty acids.

Here is Canter's method, with a few of my own modifications, which I now advocate with all enthusiasm:

1. Preheat the oven to 200°F. Warm the empty, uncoated skillet in the oven for 15 minutes, then remove the pan and turn off the oven.

2. Using paper towels, rub 2 tablespoons of flaxseed oil on the interior of the pan and the tops of the handles and then another 2 tablespoons on the exterior of the pan and the bottoms of the handles. Then take fresh paper towels and thoroughly wipe the pan all over to remove excess oil.

3. Place the pan upside down in the oven on a rack in the lowest position and heat the oven to the maximum baking temperature. In some ovens that is only 450°F, but if you can crank your oven up to 500°F or even higher, do it. *Do not put the oven on self-clean.* That setting can reach 900°F and break the skillet.

4. Bake the skillet for 1 hour. Turn off the oven and cool the pan in the oven for 3 hours.

5. Repeat the oiling, wiping, and baking (steps 2 to 4) five more times. At that point you should have a skillet with a lovely glossy patina.

Vegetarian Mexican Fideo

While the word fideo, *pronounced* fee-DAY-oh, *means* "noodle" *in Spanish, toasting the pasta is a traditional way these little bird's nests are treated. In this case the fideo are cooked with vegetables in a spicy tomato sauce and then sprinkled with salty Cotija, a cheese similar to feta.*

SERVES **4 to 6**

SIZE **12-inch skillet**

TIME **20 minutes**

Chayote, pronounced *chi-OH-tay,* is native to Latin America and is a member of the squash family. It has a mild flavor—a cross between a cucumber and an apple—and should always be peeled before cooking. It's rarely eaten raw. Zucchini is the best substitute if you can't find it.

2 cups vegetable oil

2 (7-ounce) bags coiled fideo

1 onion, diced

2 celery ribs, diced

2 large carrots, diced

2 jalapeño or serrano chiles, seeds and ribs removed, chopped

3 garlic cloves, minced

2 tablespoons ground cumin

1 tablespoon ground coriander

1 tablespoon smoked Spanish paprika

1 (½-pound) chayote squash, peeled, seeded, and cut into 1-inch pieces

3 to 4 cups tomato sauce, divided

1 cup fresh peas (or frozen peas, thawed)

Salt and freshly ground black pepper, to taste

½ cup chopped fresh cilantro, for serving

1 cup grated Cotija cheese, for serving

Place the oil in the skillet and heat it over medium-high heat. When the oil starts to shimmer, add half the fideo nests and cook them for 30 seconds per side, turning them with tongs, or until they are lightly brown. Drain the nests on paper towels and repeat with the remaining pasta.

Remove all but 2 tablespoons of the oil from the skillet. Place the skillet over medium-high heat and add the onion, celery, carrots, and chiles. Cook, stirring occasionally, for 2 minutes. Add the garlic, cumin, coriander, and paprika and cook for 1 minute, stirring constantly.

Return the pasta nests to the skillet and add the chayote and 3 cups tomato sauce. Bring to a boil, then reduce the heat to low and simmer for 5 minutes, stirring occasionally. Add more tomato sauce if it appears that the pasta has absorbed all of the sauce. Add the peas, and cook for an additional 4 minutes, or until the pasta has separated into strands and the vegetables are tender. Season with salt and pepper.

To serve, divide the pasta and vegetables into shallow bowls, and sprinkle each with cilantro and Cotija cheese.

NOTE The dish can be prepared up to 2 days in advance and refrigerated, tightly covered. Reheat it over low heat, covered, and add some water if the pasta seems dry.

VARIATION

∗ **Add ¾ pounds of boneless, skinless chicken breasts**, cut into 1-inch pieces, to the dish when adding the garlic and seasonings.

Middle Eastern Shakshuka with Baked Eggs

Middle Eastern cuisines have been growing in popularity, which is hardly surprising because many of the ingredients and flavors are so similar to the dishes from Latin American cultures. Shakshuka is a dish served at breakfast in Israel, but is usually a casual supper here. Serve some pita bread alongside.

SERVES **4 to 6**

SIZE **ovenproof 12-inch skillet**

TIME **35 minutes**

Kitchen gadgets are a boon for many tasks, but I still use my *well-washed* hands whenever possible. A lot of recipes call for whole tomatoes that are broken up rather than diced, then there's mixing ingredients for meatballs and, on the pastry side, cutting the butter into flour for piecrust. All of these tasks are easily done with your hands, so get physical with your food.

NOTE The vegetable mixture can be cooked up to 2 days in advance and refrigerated, tightly covered. Reheat it in the skillet until hot before adding and baking the eggs.

VARIATION

∗ **Add ¼ pound of crumbled feta cheese** to the vegetable sauce before adding and baking the eggs.

3 tablespoons olive oil
1 large sweet onion, such as Bermuda or Vidalia, halved and thinly sliced
4 scallions, white parts and 4 inches of green tops, sliced
1 large red bell pepper, seeds and ribs removed, thinly sliced
3 garlic cloves, minced
1 tablespoon ground cumin
2 teaspoons sweet paprika
1 (28-ounce) can whole plum tomatoes, undrained
1 to 2 tablespoons harissa, or to taste
Salt and freshly ground black pepper, to taste
4 to 6 large eggs
Chopped fresh cilantro, for serving (optional)

Preheat the oven to 375°F.

Heat the oil in the skillet over medium heat and tilt the pan around to coat it evenly. Add the onion, scallions, and pepper and cook over medium-low heat for 15 minutes, or until the vegetables soften. Add the garlic, cumin, and paprika, and cook for 30 seconds, stirring constantly.

While the vegetables cook, break up the tomatoes into smaller pieces with a pair of scissors or your fingers. Add the tomatoes and harissa to the skillet and cook over medium heat for 10 minutes, or until the mixture thickens. Season with salt and pepper.

Smooth the top of the vegetable mixture and then make 4 to 6 indentations evenly on the top with the back of a spoon. Break 1 egg into each indentation and sprinkle the eggs with salt and pepper.

Transfer the skillet to the oven and bake the eggs for 7 to 8 minutes, or until cooked to desired doneness. Sprinkle the skillet with cilantro, if using, and serve immediately.

Cod with Garbanzo Beans and Vegetables

It doesn't get much faster than this recipe to get a delicious and aromatic dinner on the table; in fact, the slicing and dicing take about the same amount of time as the cooking. Aromatic tarragon laced with tangy lemon is the dominant seasoning.

SERVES **4 to 6**

SIZE **10-inch skillet**

TIME **7 minutes**

The amount of diced tomatoes in a can, once drained, is just about 1 cup, so it's always possible to use canned in place of fresh tomatoes when they're going to be cooked. If it's the middle of winter and the cherry and grape tomatoes are looking sad in the produce department, go for a can instead.

NOTE The vegetables can be prepped up to 1 day in advance and refrigerated, tightly covered. The dish should be cooked just before serving.

VARIATION

∗ **Substitute skinless salmon fillet** or **peeled and deveined raw** shrimp (16 to 20 per pound) for the cod.

2 tablespoons olive oil
3 scallions, white parts and 4 inches of green tops, thinly sliced
½ small fennel bulb, cored and diced
1 medium zucchini, halved lengthwise and thinly sliced
¾ cup Seafood Stock (page 32) or store-bought stock
⅓ cup dry white wine
3 tablespoons chopped fresh tarragon
½ lemon, zest grated off and juiced
1 cup cherry or grape tomatoes, halved
1 (15-ounce) can garbanzo beans, drained and rinsed
1½ pounds thick cod fillet, cut into 1-inch cubes
Salt and freshly ground black pepper, to taste
Fennel fronds, for serving

Heat the oil in the skillet over medium-high heat. Add the scallions and fennel and cook for 2 minutes. Add the zucchini, stock, wine, tarragon, lemon zest, lemon juice, tomatoes, beans, and cod.

Bring to a boil over medium-high heat, then reduce the heat to low, cover the pan, and cook for 5 minutes, stirring gently a few times. Season with salt and pepper. Ladle the dish into shallow bowls, and serve immediately, garnishing each serving with fennel fronds.

Middle Eastern Shakshuka
with Baked Eggs, page 134

Japanese Shrimp and Vegetable Pancakes

(Okonomiyaki)

These pancakes are a popular form of Japanese street food; okonomi means "how you want it." Sometimes diners at casual restaurants cook them for themselves. While flavoring the batter with pickled ginger and including cabbage and scallions is traditional, you can personalize the pancakes in myriad ways. I've also made them as wonderful, miniature two-bite hors d'oeuvres by frying up a few tablespoons of the batter.

SERVES **4 to 6**

SIZE **12-inch skillet**

RESTING TIME **30 minutes**   COOKING TIME **10 minutes per batch**

While in the past decade the availability of both fresh and packaged Asian ingredients has grown dramatically, there are still some items that are difficult to find in all but large urban centers on the Pacific coast. One of these is a mountain yam called *yamaimo* in Japan. But a small amount of Yukon Gold potato adds the same creamy richness to the batter.

PANCAKES

- 1 (2-ounce) Yukon Gold potato
- 4 large eggs
- 1 cup all-purpose flour
- ¾ cup dashi (or ¾ cup hot tap water mixed with 1 tablespoon powdered dashi)
- 2 tablespoons finely chopped pickled ginger, preferably red ginger
- 2 teaspoons Japanese soy sauce
- 1 teaspoon toasted sesame oil
- ½ teaspoon sugar
- ½ teaspoon baking powder
- 1 pound peeled and deveined raw shrimp, diced
- 3 cups firmly packed shredded Napa cabbage
- ¾ cup fresh corn kernels
- 5 scallions, white parts and 6 inches of green tops, thinly sliced, with white and green portions kept separately
- 3 tablespoons vegetable oil

SAUCE AND GARNISHES

- ¼ cup ketchup
- 2 tablespoons oyster sauce
- 2 tablespoons Worcestershire sauce
- 1 tablespoon granulated sugar
- ¼ cup Japanese mayonnaise, preferably Kewpie brand
- Sliced scallion greens

Preheat the oven to 200°F and line a rimmed sheet pan with a few layers of paper towels.

Peel and dice the potato. Place it in a blender with the eggs and puree until smooth. Scrape the mixture into a mixing bowl and add the flour, dashi, pickled ginger, soy sauce, sesame oil, sugar, and baking powder. Whisk until smooth. Refrigerate the batter, covered with plastic wrap, for 30 minutes.

Remove the batter from the refrigerator, and fold in the shrimp, cabbage, corn, and white parts of scallions. Stir well to mix the ingredients.

While the batter rests, prepare the sauce. Combine the ketchup, oyster sauce, Worcestershire sauce, and sugar in a small bowl. Stir well to dissolve the sugar.

Heat 1½ tablespoons of the oil in the skillet over medium heat. Using a ½-cup measuring cup, ladle portions of the batter into the skillet, pressing them to an even thickness with a heatproof spatula. Cook for 5 minutes, or until the bottom is golden brown. Turn the pancakes gently, and cook the other side for 5 minutes. Place the cooked pancakes on the prepared baking sheet and keep them warm in the oven while frying the remaining pancakes. Use some of the remaining oil as necessary.

To serve, brush ½ tablespoon of sauce onto each pancake. Place the mayonnaise in a squeeze bottle and draw zigzag lines across the pancakes. Sprinkle each pancake with scallion greens and serve immediately.

NOTE: The pancakes can be cooked up to 1 day in advance, tightly covered and refrigerated. Reheat them in a 375°F oven for 5 to 6 minutes, or until crisp.

VARIATION

* **Substitute diced chicken** for the shrimp.

Spicy Southwest Shrimp

In addition to some heat from two forms of chiles, this hearty mélange of beans and delicate shrimp also delivers a smoky undertaste from the bacon and chipotle pepper. Serve it with some warm corn tortillas.

SERVES **4 to 6**

SIZE **12-inch skillet**

TIME **20 minutes**

Like many recipes, this one calls for 1 tablespoon of tomato paste. I buy tomato paste that comes in a tube, which will keep in the refrigerator for a few weeks. If you do use tomato paste from a can, freeze the remaining paste in 1-tablespoon portions in an ice cube tray. Then store the small cubes in a heavy plastic bag for up to 6 months.

- ¼ pound bacon, cut into thin slivers
- 1½ pounds large (16 to 20 per pound) raw shrimp, peeled and deveined
- 1 large onion, diced
- 4 garlic cloves, minced
- 2 jalapeño or serrano chiles, seeds and ribs removed, finely chopped
- 1 tablespoon ground cumin
- 2 medium ripe tomatoes, cored, seeded, and diced
- 1 (15-ounce) cans kidney beans, drained and rinsed
- 1 cup Seafood Stock (page 32), store-bought stock, or bottled clam juice
- 1 chipotle chile in adobo sauce, finely chopped
- 1 tablespoon adobo sauce
- 1 tablespoon tomato paste
- 1 teaspoon dried oregano, preferably Mexican oregano
- Salt and freshly ground black pepper, to taste
- ¼ cup chopped fresh cilantro
- Lime wedges, for serving

Heat the skillet over medium-high heat. Cook the bacon in the skillet for 5 to 7 minutes, or until crisp. Remove the bacon from the pan with a slotted spoon, and drain on paper towels. Set aside.

Pat the shrimp dry with paper towels. Discard all but 3 tablespoons of fat from the skillet and increase the heat to high. Add the shrimp and sear them on both sides. Remove the shrimp from the skillet with a slotted spoon and set aside.

Lower the heat to medium, add the onion, and cook for 2 minutes, stirring frequently. Add the garlic, jalapeños, and cumin and continue to cook for 1 minute. Add the tomatoes, beans, stock, chipotle chile, adobo sauce, tomato paste, oregano, and fried bacon to the skillet. Bring to a boil, reduce the heat to medium-low, and simmer for 10 minutes, or until the sauce thickens and is reduced by one-third.

Add the shrimp to the skillet and cook for 2 minutes, or until the shrimp are cooked through. Season with salt and pepper, and stir in the cilantro. Serve immediately, garnishing the plates with lime wedges.

NOTE The dish can be prepared, up to stirring in the cilantro, 1 day in advance. Cover it tightly and refrigerate. Reheat the dish over low heat, covered.

VARIATION

＊ **Substitute 1-inch cubes of boneless, skinless chicken thigh** for the shrimp and **substitute chicken stock** for the seafood stock. Add the chicken to the skillet at the same time as the bacon.

Shrimp Pad Thai

The beauty of cooking pad thai at home is that the plates can be artistically composed, garnished, and served piping hot. While rice noodles and many of the other ingredients in this Bangkok street food staple are now shelved in the Asian food aisle of just about all supermarkets, there are some other ingredients that remain more difficult to find. I've given substitutes for them.

SERVES **4 to 6**

SIZE **12-inch skillet**

TIME **15 minutes**

It's difficult to find prepressed tofu that is dry enough to retain its shape and doesn't fall apart when doing a stir-fried dish, even at Asian markets, but you can replicate it yourself the day before you want to use it. Start by draining a block of extra-firm tofu and cutting it in half horizontally. Pat it dry, and then lay it on a plate on top of a few layers of paper towels. Cover the tofu with another plate and then weigh it down with a brick wrapped in aluminum foil or some heavy cans of food. Refrigerate the tofu for at least 12 hours, preferably 24 hours. Change the paper towels as necessary.

- 10 ounces (¼-inch wide) rice noodles
- ¼ cup dried shrimp, chopped
- ¼ cup tamarind concentrate (substitute freshly squeezed lime juice)
- ⅓ cup palm sugar (substitute agave nectar)
- 3 tablespoons fish sauce
- 1 tablespoon Sriracha sauce, or to taste
- 1½ cups Seafood Stock (page 32) or store-bought stock
- ⅓ cup vegetable oil, divided
- 2 garlic cloves, minced
- ½ pound pressed tofu (see the sidebar on how to make your own), cut into 1-inch cubes
- 4 large eggs
- Salt and freshly ground black pepper, to taste
- 1 pound large (26 to 30 per pound) raw shrimp, peeled and deveined
- 3 scallions, white parts and 6 inches of green tops, thinly sliced on the diagonal
- 1½ cups mung bean sprouts, rinsed with roots ends removed
- ⅓ cup chopped unsalted roasted peanuts
- ½ cup firmly packed fresh Thai basil leaves, torn if large (substitute fresh cilantro leaves)
- 1 lime, cut into 4 to 6 wedges

Break the noodles into 3-inch lengths and soak them in a bowl of very hot tap water for 15 minutes, or until pliable. Drain the noodles and set them aside. Soak the dried shrimp in ½ cup very hot tap water for 15 minutes. Drain and set them aside.

Combine the tamarind, palm sugar, fish sauce, Sriracha, and stock in a mixing bowl. Whisk well to dissolve the sugar.

Heat 1 tablespoon of the oil in the skillet over medium-high heat. Add the garlic and dried shrimp and cook, stirring constantly, for 30 seconds. Remove the ingredients from the skillet and set them aside.

Heat 2 tablespoons of the oil in the skillet over medium-high heat. Add the cubes of tofu and cook them for 1 to 2 minutes, or until browned. Remove the tofu from the skillet and add it to the bowl with the garlic and dried shrimp.

Heat 2 tablespoons of the oil in the skillet over medium heat. Break the eggs into the oil and scramble them with a spatula, keeping streaks of white and yellow visible. Sprinkle the eggs with salt and pepper, and scrape them out of the skillet. Wipe the skillet with paper towels.

Heat the remaining oil in the skillet over high heat. Add the drained noodles and sauce mixture. Cook for 4 to 5 minutes, or until the sauce has almost evaporated and the noodles are sizzling. Add the shrimp and cook for 1 minute, or until the shrimp turn pink. Return the tofu and garlic mixture to the pan and cook for 30 seconds.

Divide the noodle mixture into bowls and garnish each serving with scrambled egg, scallions, bean sprouts, peanuts, and basil leaves. Serve immediately with a lime wedge.

NOTE The dish is best straight out of the skillet, but the actual cooking time is rather short if you do the slicing and dicing in advance and refrigerate your ingredients.

Greek Chicken
with Lemon and Oregano

Used together, lemon and oregano are hallmarks of Greek seasoning, and that bright combination enlivens this skillet chicken dish. Broiling the dish at the end of the cooking time gives the chicken and vegetables a crispy texture and rich brown color.

SERVES **4 to 6**

SIZE **ovenproof 12-inch skillet**

TIME **1 hour**

The length of time food marinates is determined by the nature of the food and also the composition of the marinade. For example, it takes longer for a marinade to penetrate chicken pieces with the skin on than it does to flavor skinless pieces, and the acidity of freshly squeezed lemon or lime juice penetrates food much faster than a less acidic substance like wine.

⅓ cup freshly squeezed lemon juice
1 tablespoon balsamic vinegar
5 garlic cloves, minced
2 tablespoons chopped fresh parsley
1 tablespoon dried oregano, preferably Greek
Salt and freshly ground black pepper, to taste
¼ cup olive oil, divided
4 to 6 meaty chicken thighs with bones and skin

⅔ pound baby red potatoes, halved
1 red bell pepper, seeds and ribs removed, diced
1 large onion, cut into wedges
2 small zucchini, halved lengthwise and thickly sliced
¼ cup pitted Kalamata olives, sliced
Lemon wedges, for serving
Parsley sprigs, for serving

Combine the lemon juice, vinegar, garlic, parsley, oregano, salt, and pepper in a heavy, resealable plastic bag. Mix well to dissolve the salt, then add 3 tablespoons of the olive oil and the chicken thighs. Marinate the chicken in the refrigerator for 1 hour, turning the bag occasionally.

Preheat the oven to 425°F, with the rack in the upper third of the oven. Remove the chicken from the marinade, reserving the marinade, and pat it dry with paper towels.

Heat the remaining oil in the skillet over medium-high heat. Brown the chicken well on both sides and then arrange the potatoes, bell pepper, and onion around the chicken pieces. Drizzle ¼ cup of the marinade over the vegetables and discard the remaining marinade.

Cover the skillet and bake the mixture for 20 minutes. Stir the vegetables and add the zucchini and olives to the pan. Bake for an additional 15 to 20 minutes, or until the chicken is cooked through and no longer pink, and the vegetables are tender.

Remove the skillet from the oven and preheat the oven broiler. Broil the skillet for 3 to 5 minutes, or until the chicken is crispy and browned. Serve immediately, garnishing the platter with lemon wedges and parsley sprigs.

NOTE The dish can be prepared, up to the final broiling, up to 2 days in advance and refrigerated, tightly covered. Reheat the covered dish in a 325°F oven for 15 minutes, or until hot before broiling it.

VARIATION

∗ **Substitute** 1½ pounds of **firm, white-fleshed fish, such as cod or halibut,** for the chicken thighs. Marinate the fish for only 20 minutes, and do not add the fish to the skillet until the zucchini and olives are added.

Mexican Chicken and Rice
(Arroz con Pollo)

This colorful and flavorful one-dish meal is authentically Mexican, although it was integrated into American cooking many generations ago. I serve it with sliced jicama drizzled with lime juice to add some crunch.

SERVES **4 to 6**

SIZE **12-inch skillet**

TIME **30 minutes**

Be careful when pushing your shopping cart around the Mexican section of the supermarket. Shelved right next to the mild green chiles are the jalapeño peppers, and a whole can of those would not be enjoyed by most people at the table. Trust me.

4 to 6 bone-in, skin-on chicken pieces of your choice (breasts cut in half, thighs, legs)
Salt and freshly ground black pepper, to taste
3 tablespoons olive oil
1 large onion, diced
1 green bell pepper, seeds and ribs removed, chopped
2 ounces baked ham, chopped
4 garlic cloves, minced
1½ cups long-grain white rice
2 teaspoons ground cumin
1 teaspoon dried oregano, preferably Mexican oregano

1 (14.5-ounce) can diced tomatoes, undrained
1 (4-ounce) can chopped mild green chiles, drained
1½ cups Chicken Stock (page 30) or store-bought stock
1 bay leaf
½ cup chopped pimiento-stuffed green olives
1 cup fresh green peas (or frozen peas, thawed)
¼ cup chopped fresh cilantro, for serving (optional)

Pat the chicken dry with paper towels and sprinkle the pieces with salt and pepper. Heat the oil in the skillet over medium-high heat. Add the chicken pieces, being careful not to crowd the skillet. Brown the pieces well on all sides, turning them gently with tongs. Remove the chicken from the skillet and set aside.

Add the onion, bell pepper, and ham to the skillet and cook for 3 minutes, stirring occasionally, or until the onion is translucent. Add the garlic, rice, cumin, and oregano to the skillet and cook for 2 minutes, stirring frequently.

Return the chicken to the skillet and add the tomatoes, chiles, stock, bay leaf, and olives. Bring to a boil and then lower the heat to medium-low and cook, partially covered, for 25 to 30 minutes, or until the chicken is cooked through and no longer pink and almost all the liquid has been absorbed. Stir in the peas, and cook for an additional 3 minutes. Remove and discard the bay leaf.

Serve immediately, sprinkling each serving with cilantro, if desired.

NOTE The dish can be prepared up to 2 days in advance and refrigerated, tightly covered. Reheat it in a 325°F oven for 20 to 25 minutes, or until hot.

VARIATION

✱ **Substitute boneless pork chop**s for the chicken pieces. The cooking time will remain the same.

Bacon, Egg, and Arugula Salad with Croutons

Here's a salad that you can serve at a summer brunch or as a light supper. The combination of creamy eggs, salty bacon, crunchy croutons, and peppery greens is simultaneously filling and light. The nature of the dish changes with the bread you choose to make the croutons. I've used everything from simple ciabatta to hearty herb or olive bread.

SERVES **4 to 6**

SIZE **12-inch skillet**

TIME **25 minutes**

The best way to make scrambled eggs has been a hot topic in the culinary world recently, with such authorities as Gordon Ramsay and Jamie Oliver squaring off with their methods. I think the best way to achieve fluffy and soft scrambled eggs is to cook them over low heat, covered.

DRESSING

- 1 shallot, finely chopped
- 2 garlic cloves, minced
- 2 tablespoons white wine vinegar
- 1 tablespoon Dijon mustard
- 1 tablespoon chopped fresh parsley
- 1 teaspoon fresh thyme leaves
- ½ teaspoon granulated sugar
- Salt and freshly ground black pepper, to taste
- ⅓ cup olive oil

SALAD

- ¾ pound bacon, cut into 1-inch pieces
- 4 cups ¾-inch bread cubes, preferably stale
- 2 tablespoons unsalted butter
- 10 large eggs
- ⅓ cup sour cream
- Salt and freshly ground black pepper, to taste
- 6 cups arugula leaves, rinsed and stemmed
- ½ to ¾ cup ricotta salata, crumbled, for serving

For the dressing, combine the shallot, garlic, vinegar, mustard, parsley, thyme, sugar, salt, and pepper in a jar with a tight-fitting lid, and shake well. Add the olive oil and shake well again. Set aside.

For the salad, heat the skillet over medium-high heat. Cook the bacon in the skillet for 5 to 7 minutes, or until crisp. Remove the bacon from the pan with a slotted spoon, and drain it on paper towels. Set it aside.

Add the bread cubes to the fat in the skillet and cook over medium-high heat, turning them with a slotted spatula, until brown on all sides. Remove the croutons from the skillet, drain on paper towels, and set them aside. Pour the bacon grease out of the skillet.

Melt the butter in the same skillet over low heat. Whisk the eggs with the sour cream, salt, and pepper. When the butter melts, add the eggs to the pan, then cover the pan. After 2 minutes, stir the eggs and cover the pan again. Cook until the eggs are three-quarters set.

While the eggs cook, place the arugula in a salad bowl. Toss it with ⅓ cup of the vinaigrette. Add the reserved bacon and croutons as well as the hot eggs to the salad bowl and toss gently. Serve immediately, sprinkling each serving with ricotta salata. Pass the remaining dressing separately.

NOTE The dressing can be made 2 days in advance and refrigerated, tightly covered. Bring it back to room temperature before serving. The bacon and croutons can be cooked 2 days in advance. Reheat the bacon in a microwave oven before cooking the eggs, and keep the croutons in an airtight container at room temperature.

VARIATION

* For a Mexican version of this salad, **substitute raw Mexican chorizo** for the bacon, and **fry up strips of corn tortilla** instead of bread croutons.

Chinese Pork, Wild Mushrooms, and Cellophane Noodles in Lettuce Cups

This is a variation on the dish found on the menus of myriad Asian American restaurants. The addition of wild mushrooms and cellophane noodles makes it an entrée instead of an appetizer. The dish is simply but vibrantly seasoned, and the crunchy lettuce makes it refreshing, too.

SERVES **4 to 6**

SIZE **12-inch skillet**

TIME **10 minutes**

Although the skin of fibrous ginger is very thin, you really don't want to chew it in a dish. The easiest way to peel ginger is by gently scraping it with the tip of a teaspoon. The skin comes right off and you don't waste any of the flavorful flesh.

- 6 ounces bean thread (cellophane) noodles
- 2 heads Bibb lettuce or 1 head Boston lettuce
- 3 tablespoons reduced-sodium soy sauce
- 2 tablespoons Chinese oyster sauce
- 2 tablespoons Chinese rice wine or dry sherry
- 3 tablespoons vegetable oil, divided
- 3 tablespoons minced fresh ginger
- 3 garlic cloves, minced
- 1 small jalapeño or serrano chile, seeds and ribs removed, finely chopped
- 6 ounces fresh shiitake mushrooms, stemmed and thinly sliced
- 1 pound lean ground pork
- 2 teaspoons toasted sesame oil
- Salt and freshly ground black pepper, to taste
- 4 scallions, white parts and 6 inches of green tops, thinly sliced on the diagonal

Soak the noodles in a bowl of very hot tap water for 15 minutes, or until pliable. Drain well, cut the noodles into 2-inch lengths with scissors, and set them aside. Separate the lettuce into leaves, cutting them in half if they're larger than a few bites. Rinse and dry the lettuce and arrange the leaves on a platter.

Combine the soy sauce, oyster sauce, and rice wine in a small bowl and stir well.

Heat 2 tablespoons of the oil in the skillet over high heat. Add the ginger, garlic, and chile and stir-fry for 30 seconds. Add the drained noodles and stir-fry for 2 minutes. Add the remaining oil and the mushrooms. Cook for 2 minutes.

Crumble the pork into the skillet and cook for 3 to 4 minutes, breaking up lumps with a fork, or until the pork has lost its pink color. Stir in the sauce mixture and sesame oil and cook for 2 minutes. Season with salt and pepper and scrape the mixture into a serving bowl. Sprinkle the scallions over the top and serve immediately, wrapping up portions of the mixture in the lettuce leaves.

NOTE This dish can be prepared up to 1 day in advance and refrigerated, tightly covered. Reheat it over low heat or in a microwave-safe dish.

VARIATION

⁎ **Substitute ground dark turkey meat** for the pork.

Creamy Swedish Meatballs with Egg Noodles and Vegetables

Not all one-pot pasta recipes in this book call for one of the myriad Italian shapes. Homey egg noodles are the perfect foil to the creamy sauce flecked with aromatic fresh dill in this dish that pleases all generations.

SERVES **4 to 6**

SIZE **12-inch skillet**

TIME **25 minutes**

Fresh herbs often go to waste if a recipe doesn't require the use of the whole bunch. Herbs such as dill and parsley can be frozen successfully for future use, however. Just rinse small amounts of the herb, pat them dry with paper towels, and then bundle and tightly wrap them with plastic wrap. You can "chop" the herbs with the dull side of a chef's knife when you pull them out of the freezer.

4 tablespoons (½ stick) unsalted butter, divided
1 large shallot, minced
2 garlic cloves, minced (optional)
½ cup panko breadcrumbs
⅓ cup whole milk
¼ teaspoon freshly grated nutmeg
¾ pound ground pork
¾ pound ground veal
Salt and freshly ground black pepper, to taste

3 tablespoons all-purpose flour
1½ cups Chicken Stock (page 30) or store-bought stock
¾ cup whole milk
½ cup heavy cream
⅓ cup chopped fresh dill
2 carrots, thinly sliced
2 ounces fresh green beans, cut into 1-inch pieces
6 ounces wide egg noodles
Sprigs of fresh dill, for serving

Melt 1 tablespoon of the butter in the skillet over low heat. Add the shallot and cook, stirring frequently, for 2 minutes. Add the garlic, if using, and cook for 1 minute, or until the shallot softens. Scrape the mixture into a large mixing bowl, and allow it to cool.

Add the breadcrumbs, milk, and nutmeg to the mixing bowl and whisk until smooth. Add the pork and veal, and mix well. Season with salt and pepper, and form the mixture into meatballs about the size of walnuts.

Melt 1 tablespoon of the remaining butter in the skillet over medium-high heat. Add the meatballs and brown them lightly on all sides, turning them gently with tongs. Remove the meatballs from the skillet and set them aside. Wipe the skillet with paper towels.

Melt the remaining butter in the skillet. Stir in the flour and cook, stirring constantly, for 1 minute, or until the mixture turns slightly beige, is bubbly, and appears to have grown in volume. Increase the heat to medium and slowly whisk in the stock, milk, and cream. Bring to a boil, whisking frequently. Reduce the heat to low, and simmer the sauce for 2 minutes.

Return the meatballs to the skillet and add the dill and carrots. Simmer the mixture for 5 minutes over medium heat. Add the green beans and egg noodles, and return the mixture to a boil. Cook an additional 6 minutes over low heat, uncovered, or until the egg noodles are al dente and the vegetables are tender. Season with salt and pepper and serve immediately, garnishing the plates with sprigs of fresh dill.

NOTE The dish can be cooked up to 2 days in advance and refrigerated, tightly covered. Reheat it in a 350°F oven for 10 to 15 minutes, covered, and add additional stock or milk if the dish needs thinning once reheated.

Pan-Fried Gnocchi
with Sausage and Mushrooms

I am a great fan of gnocchi, probably because I've never met a potato I didn't like, so when you add them to pasta dough and cook them as fluffy little pillows, I'm in heaven. This dish brings them together in a flavorful, creamy tomato sauce with Parmesan, sausage, mushrooms, and other vegetables. A crunchy tossed salad is a nice contrast to the satiny texture of the dish.

SERVES **4 to 6**

SIZE **12-inch skillet**

TIME **18 to 20 minutes**

While bulk sausage is usually easy to find, there have been times that I've had to buy links instead. It's really important to remove the sausage meat and discard the casings. If you just slice the raw sausage, the bits of casing will separate from the meat as it cooks, and chewing the casing is akin to munching on rubber bands.

¼ cup olive oil, divided

¾ pound potato gnocchi, thawed if frozen

1 pound bulk Italian sausage (sweet or hot), made from either pork or poultry

1 onion, diced

¼ pound mushrooms, sliced

3 garlic cloves, minced

1 (14.5-ounce) can diced tomatoes, undrained

½ cup Chicken Stock (page 30) or store-bought stock

¼ cup firmly packed sliced fresh basil

2 tablespoons chopped fresh parsley

¼ cup heavy cream

½ cup freshly grated Parmesan cheese

Salt, to taste

Crushed red pepper flakes, to taste

Fresh basil leaves, for serving

Heat 2 tablespoons of the oil in the skillet over medium heat. Add the gnocchi and cook them for 3 minutes, or until brown on both sides, turning them gently with a spatula. Remove the gnocchi from the skillet with a slotted spoon and set them aside.

Add the remaining oil to the skillet and crumble in the sausage. Cook for 2 minutes, stirring occasionally. Add the onion and mushrooms and cook, stirring frequently, for 5 minutes. Add the garlic and cook for 1 minute, or until the onions and mushrooms have softened.

Return the gnocchi to the skillet and add the tomatoes, stock, basil, and parsley. Bring to a boil, reduce the heat to low, cover the pan, and cook for 3 to 5 minutes, or until the gnocchi are cooked through; the amount of time varies with the brand of gnocchi.

Uncover the skillet and stir in the cream and Parmesan. Cook for 2 minutes, or until the cheese melts and the sauce thickens. Season with salt and crushed red pepper flakes, garnish the plates with basil leaves, and serve immediately.

NOTE The vegetable and sausage mixture can be prepared 1 day in advance and refrigerated, tightly covered. Reheat it over low heat, covered, before cooking the gnocchi and finishing the dish.

Kofta Meatballs with
Dilled Rice and Tzatziki Sauce

The addition of fresh zucchini and the punctuation provided by vibrant cherry tomatoes turn this meatball and rice dish into a full meal. While there's a lot of flavor in the dish already, I like to pass around a bowl of creamy and crunchy tzatziki sauce with it, in keeping with the Greek inspiration.

SERVES **4 to 6**

SIZE **ovenproof 12-inch skillet**

TIME **30 minutes**

If time permits, I prefer to use drained plain whole milk yogurt to Greek style; it achieves a silkier texture. Line a fine-meshed sieve with a double layer of cheesecloth and place 2 cups of plain whole milk yogurt in it. Refrigerate the yogurt overnight and then discard the whey from the mixing bowl. You'll have just the right amount of "yogurt cheese" needed for this sauce.

DISH

- ¼ cup plain breadcrumbs
- 1 large egg, lightly beaten
- 2 tablespoons tomato juice
- 1¼ pounds ground lamb
- 1 large shallot, minced
- 3 garlic cloves, minced
- ¼ cup chopped fresh parsley
- 1 tablespoon ground coriander
- 2 teaspoons ground cumin
- 1 teaspoon dried oregano, preferably Greek
- ¼ teaspoon ground cinnamon
- ¼ teaspoon cayenne
- ¼ teaspoon ground ginger
- Salt and freshly ground black pepper, to taste
- 2 tablespoons olive oil
- 1½ cups long-grain white rice
- 3 cups Chicken Stock (page 30) or store-bought stock
- ¼ cup chopped fresh dill
- 1 teaspoon grated lemon zest
- 2 tablespoons freshly squeezed lemon juice
- 2 medium zucchini, halved lengthwise and thinly sliced
- 1 cup cherry tomatoes, halved (or quartered if large)

SAUCE

- 1 medium cucumber, peeled, halved lengthwise, and seeded
- 1 cup Greek-style whole milk plain yogurt
- 1 garlic clove, minced
- 1 tablespoon freshly squeezed lemon juice
- 2 teaspoons white wine vinegar
- 2 tablespoons chopped fresh dill
- Pinch of salt
- Freshly ground white pepper, to taste

Combine the breadcrumbs, egg, and tomato juice in a mixing bowl and allow the mixture to sit for 5 minutes. Add the lamb, shallot, garlic, parsley, coriander, cumin, oregano, cinnamon, cayenne, ginger, salt, and pepper and mix well. Refrigerate the mixture for 15 minutes to allow the flavors to blend.

(continued on the following page)

(continued from the previous page)

Preheat the oven to 375°F.

Form the meat into oval shapes about 2½ to 3 inches long. Heat the oil in the skillet over medium-high heat. Brown the meatballs on all sides, turning them gently with tongs. Remove the meatballs from the skillet and set aside.

Add the rice to the skillet and cook for 2 minutes, stirring constantly. Add the stock, dill, lemon zest, and lemon juice to the skillet and bring to a boil over medium heat. Return the meatballs to the skillet, cover the skillet, and bake for 15 minutes.

While the dish is baking, prepare the sauce. Grate the cucumber through the large holes of a box grater. Drain the pieces in a fine-meshed sieve and then wring them out in a clean tea towel. Place the cucumber in a mixing bowl and add the yogurt, garlic, lemon juice, vinegar, dill, salt, and pepper. Stir well and refrigerate until ready to serve.

Add the zucchini and tomatoes to the skillet and return it to the oven for 10 minutes, or until the vegetables are cooked and the rice has absorbed all the liquid. Season with salt and pepper and serve immediately, passing around the sauce separately.

NOTE The dish can be prepared up to 2 days in advance and refrigerated, tightly covered. Reheat it, covered, in a 350°F oven for 20 to 25 minutes, or until hot.

VARIATION

* **Substitute ground beef or a combination of beef, veal, and pork** for the ground lamb.

Skillet Pasta Puttanesca

This boldly flavored dish hails from Naples. There are many rumors about the origin of the name, most of them probably apocryphal. The most popular is that brothel elders would cook this dish to lure customers inside. The sauce is simple and depends on bold ingredients like anchovies, black olives, crushed red pepper flakes, and garlic to make the tomato sauce zing. Serve the Pasta Puttanesca with a tossed salad.

SERVES **4 to 6**

SIZE **12-inch skillet**

TIME **15 minutes**

The way you treat garlic determines the intensity of its flavor. Pushing the cloves through a garlic press is the way to extract the most punch. Mincing the cloves once they're peeled produces a milder flavor.

NOTE If cooking the dish in advance, reduce the second cooking time to 4 minutes and then bring it back to a boil to finish cooking just prior to serving.

VARIATION

∗ **Substitute 1 (28-ounce) can whole plum tomatoes,** drained and crushed with a fork or your hands, for the fresh tomatoes.

3 tablespoons olive oil
1 onion, diced
4 anchovy fillets, mashed
½ teaspoon crushed red pepper flakes, or to taste
4 garlic cloves, minced
¼ cup tomato paste
4 cups Chicken Stock (page 30) or store-bought stock
1 pound dried linguine or bucatini
3 pints cherry or grape tomatoes, halved
¼ cup chopped fresh basil
3 tablespoons chopped fresh parsley
2 tablespoons chopped fresh oregano
½ cup oil-cured black olives, pitted and diced
2 tablespoons capers, drained and rinsed
Salt and freshly ground black pepper, to taste
Freshly grated Parmesan cheese, for serving

Heat the oil in the skillet over medium-high heat. Add the onion, anchovies, and crushed red pepper flakes and cook, stirring frequently, for 2 minutes. Add the garlic, and cook for 1 minute, stirring constantly. Stir in the tomato paste and stock, and bring to a boil, stirring well to dissolve the tomato paste.

Add the pasta, reduce the heat to medium, and simmer the pasta, uncovered, for 6 minutes. Add the tomatoes, basil, parsley, oregano, olives, and capers and cook for an additional 6 to 8 minutes, or until the pasta is al dente and the sauce has reduced. Season with salt and pepper and serve immediately, passing the cheese separately.

chapter 6

Sheet Pans

The sheet pan has become one of the most versatile pieces of equipment in the kitchen. You've always used sheet pans to bake cookies or breads, and now cooks are using them as low-sided roasting pans to ensure that all elements of a meal are baked together. And when the meal has been eaten, the foil covering the sheet pan is thrown out and voilà! There's literally nothing to scrub and scour.

While there are recipes in Chapter 7 that need the higher sides of a roasting pan to work successfully, one of the benefits of a sheet pan is that the low sides allow food to brown and become crispy without any need to fiddle or stir ingredients.

Cooking savory foods on sheet pans is also popular in the United Kingdom and countries of the British Commonwealth, where the dishes are known as "tray bakes."

The sheet pan typically used in a home kitchen is actually a half-sheet pan, 13 × 18 inches, with a 1- to 1½-inch lip, rather than the standard 18 × 26 inches of a full commercial sheet pan. A commercial sheet pan is too large to fit in most home ovens. One benefit of standardized sheet pan sizes is that standardized wire racks fit them perfectly. The racks can be used for cooling baked goods, but they're also used to raise food above the pan so hot air can surround it on all sides.

The best sheet pans are shiny and made from aluminum or occasionally an aluminum alloy. And unlike Dutch ovens or roasting pans, sheet pans are relatively inexpensive. It's possible to find sturdy ones for less than $15, and it's difficult to spend more than $20 on one.

The most important aspect of choosing a sheet pan is to make sure it feels sturdy and doesn't bend in any way. The high oven heat used to prepare many sheet pan dishes has a tendency to warp thin pans.

midway through the cooking process. Heat rises, so the food in the pan on the top shelf has more opportunity to brown than the food than on the lower shelf.

Sheet pan versus cookie sheets: while a sheet pan can be used to bake cookies, a cookie pan cannot be used for savory recipes that cause any amount of moisture to form. Sheet pans are standardized in size because home versions were developed from commercial products. But cookie sheet sizes are all over the map. They range in size from 10 × 12 inches to grand ones that are 16 × 20 inches. Some of them have very low sides, but most have a lip only on one side to make it easier to get them in and out of the oven.

Reversing the Position

While many recipes in this chapter are baked on one sheet pan, others require two pans to allow enough space on the pan so that foods brown and don't steam. Even with a convection fan running, it's important to reverse the positions of the sheet pans

Cooking en Papillote

Just as hemlines rise and fall on women's skirts and men's ties vary in width, cooking methods go in and out of vogue. But the reason for their resurgence in popularity frequently changes with the times.

Cooking food en papillote, which literally means "in parchment" in French, started out in restaurants decades ago because it was a showy means of presentation, although steaming was already common. Cooking en papillote, pronounced *ehn pah-pee-yoht*, was then plucked from relative obscurity to take its place in the healthy eating movement that began in the 1980s, primarily because the method requires very little fat to be successful. We're returning to it now because at the end of the meal the packets are tossed in the trash and there's no cleanup required—none at all. To ensure that there's nothing to wash after eating, I line the sheet pans with aluminum foil. If there's no leakage from the pouches of food the foil can be reused.

When food is sealed in a small environment like a pouch, it cooks in its own juices, and it cooks quickly because it's surrounded by moist heat. As the packages heat, the air inside expands, which is why parchment puffs.

Cooking delicate fish en papillote is the most common use of the technique, but it also works very well for boneless, skinless chicken. It's possible to braise meats in individual packets, too. They must cook much longer, and at a lower temperature, but it does work. In Italian the method is called *in cartoccio*, which means "in a bag," and in some Asian cultures banana leaves are used as non-edible wrappers.

We've also learned that while heart-shaped sheets of parchment are dramatic, it's much quicker and easier to substitute rectangles made with aluminum foil. It creates a tighter seal with less effort than folding parchment, and aluminum foil is something that we all have in our kitchens.

While it's possible that acidic ingredients such as tomatoes or citrus juices might react to the aluminum and give food a "tinny" flavor, the cooking times for the recipes are so short that I've not experienced that as a problem. Foil stands up to heat, but parchment packages need to be brushed with water before they're baked or they'll brown too rapidly and may crumble.

Here's how to deal with parchment if you're a purist: Cut out sheets of parchment paper that are 15 × 24 inches, and fold each in half to form a 12 × 15-inch rectangle. Draw a half heart shape on each rectangle, centering it on the folded edge, and cut out each heart. Coat the inside of the parchment with softened butter or oil to keep food from sticking, leaving a 2-inch border untreated. Once the food is assembled, fold one half of the heart over and line up the edges. Starting at the top of the heart, fold down about ½ inch of the edge, pressing down to make a crisp crease.

Continue working your way around the edge of the packet, making overlapping folds that resemble pleats. Press firmly so that the folds hold; twist the tip of the heart to finish.

Parchment paper has been treated with an acid and coated with silicone, similar to silicone baking sheet liners. The coating makes it sturdy and burn-resistant, and it prevents liquids from seeping out. Never substitute wax paper for parchment paper, and never bake parchment paper at a temperature above 450°F.

If you're using aluminum foil, leave it as a 12 × 15-inch rectangle, but do grease the inside of the packet. To seal the packet firmly, crimp the edges.

Another great benefit to cooking en papillote is that the packages can be assembled up to 1 day in advance and refrigerated, unless they contain ingredients such as slices of apple or potato that may discolor. And the cooking time is so short that it makes these dishes great candidates for entertaining on work nights.

Stuffed Peppers

I love stuffed vegetables—and bell peppers are such a natural because they're the right size for a complete meal. In this vegetarian version, the sweet flesh of the pepper is countered by salty feta and aromatic fresh dill.

SERVES **4 to 6**

SIZE **13 × 18-inch half-sheet pan**

TIME **35 minutes**

A bonus of cooking peppers on a sheet pan is that the flesh becomes uniformly tender, but a possible negative is that it is easy for the peppers to fall over, because the sides of the pan are quite low. That's why it is important to shave off the bottom of each pepper so that it sits firmly on the pan.

NOTE The pepper filling can be prepared up to 2 days in advance and refrigerated, tightly covered. Do not stuff or bake the peppers until just before serving.

VARIATION

∗ **Add** 1 (5-ounce) can **light tuna** packed in olive oil, well drained, to the filling.

3 tablespoons olive oil
1½ cups Israeli couscous
4 to 6 red bell peppers
2 cups Vegetable Stock (page 33) or store-bought stock
2 tablespoons freshly squeezed lemon juice
¼ pound baby spinach leaves
2 tablespoons chopped fresh dill
¾ cup crumbled feta cheese
Salt and freshly ground black pepper, to taste
Dill sprigs, for serving

Preheat the oven to 425°F. Place a rack in the middle of the oven and line the sheet pan with heavy-duty aluminum foil.

Drizzle the olive oil over the couscous and spread it out on the sheet pan. Bake the couscous for 5 to 7 minutes, or until lightly browned. Remove the couscous from the oven and reduce the oven temperature to 375°F.

Cut the caps off of the red peppers, about ½ inch below the stems, and remove and discard the seeds and ribs. Cut a shallow slice off the bottom of each pepper so that it sits firmly and flatly on the sheet pan, being careful not to slice into the main cavity. Discard the stem and chop the flesh of the cap and the bottom slices.

Heat the stock in the microwave until hot but not boiling. Place it in a mixing bowl and add the toasted couscous, chopped pepper flesh, lemon juice, spinach leaves, dill, and feta. Season with salt and pepper and divide the mixture into the peppers.

Arrange the peppers on the sheet pan and bake them for 35 to 40 minutes, or until the couscous has absorbed the liquid. Serve hot, garnishing each one with a dill sprig.

Eggplant Parmesan

You'll be amazed at how delightful the crispy slices of eggplant are in this easy version of the Italian American classic. Rather than frying the eggplant slices, they're baked on a sheet pan, and then each slice is topped individually with sauce and cheese. A tossed salad with a garlicky Italian dressing completes the meal.

SERVES **4 to 6**

SIZE **13 × 18-inch half-sheet pan**

TIME **40 minutes**

Authentic Italian mozzarella is dubbed *di bufala* because it's made from the milk of the water buffalo, which is very high in fat and not easily digestible. It also costs about three times as much as cow's milk, which is why the cheese comes with such a hefty price tag in American supermarkets. Cow's milk mozzarella—*fior di latte*—is made with whole milk. Do not substitute part-skim mozzarella, because it does not melt as well.

1½ pounds of eggplant, preferably Italian
½ cup kosher salt plus additional for seasoning
2 large eggs
2 garlic cloves, minced
Freshly ground black pepper, to taste
1 cup plain panko breadcrumbs
¾ cup freshly grated Parmesan cheese, divided
2 teaspoons dried Italian seasoning
¼ cup olive oil
2 cups prepared marinara sauce (homemade or store-bought)
1½ cups shredded whole milk mozzarella cheese
½ cup chopped fresh basil

Preheat the oven to 400°F. Place the rack in the middle of the oven and line a sheet pan with heavy-duty aluminum foil.

Discard the cap of the eggplant, and cut it into ¾-inch slices. Combine ½ cup of the kosher salt with 1 quart of cold water in a mixing bowl and add the eggplant slices. Soak the eggplant in the salted water for 10 minutes, pressing the slices down into the brine with a plate. Drain the slices, and use a towel to absorb as much water as possible.

Whisk the eggs and garlic in a shallow bowl and season the mixture with salt and pepper. Combine the panko, ½ cup of the Parmesan, and the Italian seasoning in another bowl. Dip the eggplant slices into the egg, allowing any excess to drip off, and then dredge them in the seasoned breadcrumbs.

Spread the olive oil onto the prepared sheet pan and heat it for 3 minutes in the preheated oven. Remove it carefully and arrange the eggplant slices on top of the hot oil. Bake the slices for 20 minutes. Turn the slices with a slotted spatula and top each slice with marinara sauce and mozzarella cheese. Sprinkle the remaining Parmesan and the basil on top.

Bake for an additional 15 minutes, or until the cheese is melted and bubbly. Serve immediately.

NOTE The eggplant can be prepared for baking up to 1 day in advance and refrigerated, tightly covered.

VARIATION

* **Place a slice of prosciutto** on the eggplant slices on top of the sauce and under the cheeses.

Mexican Cod Tacos with Tomatillos

Fish tacos are a specialty of Southern California, and the tart acidity of tomatillos is a great balance to the delicate flavor of the cod. The vibrant sauce drizzled over the fish enlivens the whole dish. Serve these tacos with refried beans.

SERVES **4 to 6**

SIZE **13 × 18-inch half-sheet pan**

TIME **20 to 30 minutes**

Flour tortillas come in a variety of sizes, up to 12 inches in diameter, but corn tortillas are very rarely larger than 6 inches. Flour tortillas can be rolled and pressed larger because they contain gluten. Corn tortillas are gluten-free, and they fall apart if made too large. While flour tortillas are just a wrapper, corn tortillas add their distinctive flavor to dishes. They work beautifully with the tomatillo tartness in this dish.

- 1½ pounds small tomatillos
- 1 large red onion, thinly sliced
- ½ cup olive oil, divided
- 4 to 6 (4-ounce) cod fillets
- ¾ cup chopped fresh cilantro, divided
- 3 tablespoons snipped fresh chives
- Salt and freshly ground black pepper, to taste
- 1 lime, thinly sliced with seeds discarded
- 6 scallions, white parts and 4 inches of green tops, chopped
- ¼ cup freshly squeezed lime juice
- 1 or 2 jalapeño or serrano chiles, seeds and ribs removed, finely chopped
- 2 tablespoons Asian fish sauce
- 8 to 12 (6-inch) corn tortillas, warmed

Preheat the oven to 375°F. Place the rack in the middle of the oven and line a sheet pan with heavy-duty aluminum foil.

Remove the husks from the tomatillos and rinse them to remove the sticky residue. Cut the tomatillos into ½-inch-thick slices.

Place the tomatillos and onion slices on the baking pan and toss them with 3 tablespoons of the oil. Rub the tops of the fish fillets with the remaining oil and place the pieces on top of the vegetables. Sprinkle with ¼ cup of the cilantro and the chives, and season with salt and pepper. Lay the lime slices on top of the fish. Bake for 10 to 15 minutes, or until the fish flakes easily.

While the fish bakes, combine the remaining cilantro, remaining olive oil, scallions, lime juice, chiles, and fish sauce in a small bowl. Stir well and set aside.

Remove the pan from the oven and increase the temperature to 475°F. Remove the fish from the baking sheet, discard the lime slices, and place the fish on a platter, covering loosely with aluminum foil to keep it warm. Return the tomatillos and onions to the oven and cook for 10 minutes, or until the onions are slightly charred.

To serve, break the fish apart into bite-sized pieces and arrange them in the warmed tortillas. Drizzle the sauce over the fish and top with a portion of the tomatillo mixture. Serve immediately.

NOTE Do not make this dish more than 2 hours in advance, but if you must make it a little bit ahead, reheat it for 5 to 7 minutes in a 325°F oven.

VARIATION

∗ **Boneless, skinless chicken breasts**, cut into 1-inch strips, can be substituted for the fish.

Salmon with Summer Vegetables en Papillote

This dish is as visually stunning as it is delicious. The mélange of vegetables becomes a colorful base for a blushing pink fillet of salmon, and everything is flavored with fresh herbs. It's in the oven for such a short time that the kitchen doesn't heat up, either.

SERVES **4 to 6**

SIZE **2 (13 × 18-inch) half-sheet pans**

TIME **8 to 10 minutes**

The best way to handle fresh herbs is to treat them like a bouquet of flowers. Trim the stems when you bring them in from the market and then stand them up in a glass in which you've poured a few inches of water. Either refrigerated or sitting on the counter, they'll stay fresh and flavorful.

2 tablespoons olive oil
1½ cups fresh corn kernels
1 cup halved cherry tomatoes
¼ pound green beans, trimmed and cut into 1-inch lengths
1 small zucchini, halved lengthwise and thinly sliced
2 tablespoons chopped fresh tarragon
1 tablespoon fresh thyme leaves
3 tablespoons chopped fresh parsley, divided

4 tablespoons (½ stick) unsalted butter, divided
Kosher salt and freshly ground black pepper, to taste
4 to 6 (4- to 6-ounce) skinless salmon fillets, about ¾-inch thick
3 tablespoons dry white wine

Preheat the oven to 400°F. Place the racks in the upper third and middle positions and line 2 large rimmed sheet pans with heavy-duty aluminum foil. Prepare the desired number of hearts of parchment paper or rectangles of aluminum foil as directed on page 163, and brush the interior of the pouches with the olive oil.

Combine the corn, tomatoes, green beans, zucchini, tarragon, thyme, and 1 tablespoon of the parsley in a mixing bowl. Melt 3 tablespoons of the butter and add it to the bowl with the vegetables. Season with salt and pepper, and toss to coat the vegetables evenly.

Divide the vegetable mixture among the pouches and top with a portion of the salmon. Season the salmon with salt and pepper, and sprinkle with the remaining parsley. Cut the remaining butter into thin slices and place them on top of the salmon, and drizzle the wine on top of the butter. Seal the pouches as described on page 163.

Arrange the pouches on the baking sheets. Bake them for 4 minutes, reverse the positions in the oven, and bake for an additional 4 to 6 minutes, or until the pouches are puffed.

Remove the pouches from the oven. Cut them open with scissors, taking care when opening the pouches to avoid being burned by the hot steam. Serve immediately.

NOTE The pouches can be prepared for baking up to 1 day in advance and refrigerated. Bake them just prior to serving.

VARIATION

* **Substitute thin slices of boneless, skinless chicken breast** for the salmon.

Chinese Shrimp, Vegetables, and Rice Noodles en Papillote

You'll find that vibrant Asian flavors are perfect for cooking en papillote, and the shrimp will be perfectly cooked while the vegetables remain crisp-tender. The addition of thin rice noodles completes the package.

SERVES **4 to 6**

SIZE **2 (13 × 18-inch) half-sheet pans**

TIME **8 to 10 minutes**

To devein a shrimp means to remove the intestinal tract, which appears as a black vein. The first step is the easy part: pull off the shell. Keep the shrimp shells in the freezer—they're great for making stock. To devein a shrimp, hold it curved around one hand so you can see the vein on its back. Cut a slit with the tip of a sharp paring knife and pull out the black vein. Depending on where the shrimp are caught, some hardly need this process.

2 tablespoons vegetable oil

7 ounces rice vermicelli noodles

2 tablespoons soy sauce

2 tablespoons unseasoned rice wine vinegar

2 tablespoons hoisin sauce

1 tablespoon freshly squeezed lime juice

1 tablespoon Sriracha sauce, or to taste

1 tablespoon honey

1 tablespoon toasted sesame oil

1 tablespoon minced fresh ginger

2 garlic cloves, minced

1½ pounds large (16 to 20 per pound) raw shrimp, peeled and deveined

½ pound bok choy, cut into ¾-inch thick slices on the diagonal

1 celery rib, cut into ½-inch thick slices on the diagonal

3 ounces fresh shiitake mushrooms, stemmed and sliced

2 scallions, white parts and 4 inches of green tops, thinly sliced, for serving

Preheat the oven to 400°F. Place the racks in the upper third and middle positions of the oven, and line 2 sheet pans with heavy-duty aluminum foil. Prepare the desired number of hearts of parchment paper or rectangles of aluminum foil as directed on page 163, and brush the interior of the pouches with the vegetable oil.

Place the rice vermicelli in a mixing bowl and cover it with very hot tap water. Soak the noodles for 5 minutes, or until pliable. Rinse the noodles under cold running water, drain well, and set them aside.

Combine the soy sauce, vinegar, hoisin sauce, lime juice, Sriracha, honey, sesame oil, ginger, and garlic in a small bowl and stir well. Combine the shrimp, bok choy, celery, and mushrooms in a mixing bowl. Add the sauce and toss.

Divide the noodles into the pouches and top with a portion of the shrimp and vegetables. Seal the pouches as described on page 163.

Arrange the pouches on the baking sheets. Bake them for 4 minutes, reverse the positions in the oven, and bake for an additional 4 to 6 minutes, or until the pouches are puffed.

Remove the pouches from the oven, cut them open with scissors, and take care when opening the pouches to avoid being burned by the hot steam. Sprinkle each serving with scallions and serve immediately.

NOTE The pouches can be prepared for baking up to 1 day in advance and refrigerated. Bake them just prior to serving.

VARIATION

* **Substitute 1½ pounds firm, white-fleshed fish fillet** such as cod or halibut, cut into 1-inch cubes, for the shrimp.

Crispy Fish Tacos

A large part of Mexico is coastline, so it's not surprising that fish and seafood play such an important role in the cuisine. The crunch in these tacos comes from a combination of Japanese panko breadcrumbs and pine nuts, and the mayonnaise dip that adheres them to the tender fish is seasoned to provide some spice.

SERVES **4 to 6**

SIZE **13 × 18-inch half-sheet pan**

TIME **25 minutes**

Cholula is a Mexican hot sauce that is native to the Jalisco region. Now owned by tequila giant Jose Cuervo, the sauce is a key ingredient in sangrita, a blend of citrus juices used as a chaser for shots of tequila. Cholula wasn't introduced in the United States until 1989, but it soon became the darling of Mexican food aficionados. The ingredients are a combination of pequín and arbol chiles blended with spices and vinegar.

- 2 cups panko breadcrumbs
- ½ cup pine nuts
- Salt and freshly ground black pepper, to taste
- 1½ pounds (¾-inch-thick) firm-fleshed fish fillets, such as scrod, halibut, or striped bass
- 2 large eggs
- ⅓ cup mayonnaise
- 2 tablespoons chili powder
- 2 teaspoons ground cumin
- 1 tablespoon Mexican hot sauce, such as Cholula, divided
- 2 garlic cloves, minced
- Vegetable oil spray
- 12 (6-inch) corn tortillas
- ½ cup sour cream
- 2 tablespoons freshly squeezed lime juice
- Sliced avocado, for serving
- Sprigs of fresh cilantro, for serving
- Shredded jicama, for serving
- Lime wedges, for serving

Preheat the oven to 350°F. Place the rack in the upper third of the oven and line a sheet pan with heavy-duty aluminum foil.

Combine the panko and pine nuts in a heavy, resealable plastic bag. Crush the mixture with the flat side of a meat mallet or the bottom of a small skillet. Transfer the crumbs to the baking sheet and bake for 10 to 12 minutes, or until lightly browned. Transfer the mixture to a plate and season with salt and pepper. Wipe off the sheet pan with a paper towel.

While the crumbs are baking, cut the fish fillets into 1-inch-wide strips. Combine the eggs, mayonnaise, chili powder, cumin, 1 teaspoon of the hot sauce, garlic, and additional salt and pepper in a mixing bowl, and whisk until smooth.

(continued on the following page)

(continued from the previous page)

Place a wire cooling rack on the sheet pan, and grease it with vegetable oil spray. Dip the fish pieces in the mayonnaise mixture and then roll and press them gently into the crumbs, to help them adhere to the fish. Arrange the fish on the wire rack.

Bake the fish for 15 to 18 minutes, or until it flakes easily. Soften the corn tortillas by wrapping them in foil and baking them during the last 10 minutes that the fish is in the oven. While the fish bakes, combine the remaining hot sauce, sour cream, and lime juice in a bowl and stir well.

To serve, divide the fish among the tortillas and pass around bowls with the sour cream sauce, avocado, cilantro, jicama, and lime wedges.

NOTE The fish can be prepared for baking up to 6 hours in advance and refrigerated, tightly covered with plastic wrap.

VARIATION

∗ **Substitute strips of boneless, skinless chicken breast or chicken thigh** for the fish and increase the baking time to 25 minutes, or until the chicken is cooked through and no longer pink.

Herbed Vegetables en Papillote

I've fed this dish, as an appetizer, to six guests, and it's enough for four main dish servings, too. The vegetables remain crisp-tender and retain all their nutrients, because they exude all the moisture that is needed to cook them.

SERVES **4 to 6**

SIZE **2 (13 × 18-inch) half-sheet pans**

TIME **20 minutes**

When developing recipes to cook en papillote, the key to success is the size of the pieces. Harder foods must be cut into smaller pieces than softer foods, because once the packages are sealed you can't open them to poke, prod, add, or subtract ingredients. That's why the carrots and potatoes in this recipe should be much more thinly sliced than the leeks and squash, and the asparagus can be left whole.

NOTE The pouches can be prepared for baking up to 4 hours in advance and refrigerated. Bake them just prior to serving.

VARIATION

∗ **Haricots verts can be substituted** for the asparagus, and chopped fresh tarragon can be substituted for the oregano.

2 tablespoons vegetable oil
2 carrots, very thinly sliced
½ pound fingerling or new potatoes, very thinly sliced
1 large leek, white and pale green part, halved lengthwise, sliced, and rinsed well
1 medium yellow squash, halved lengthwise and sliced
3 tablespoons unsalted butter, melted
3 tablespoons chopped fresh oregano
2 tablespoons chopped fresh parsley
Salt and freshly ground black pepper, to taste
1 pound thin asparagus spears, trimmed (slice vertically if thicker than a pencil)

Preheat the oven to 400°F. Place the racks in the upper third and middle positions of the oven, and line 2 sheet pans with heavy-duty aluminum foil. Prepare the desired number of hearts of parchment paper or rectangles of aluminum foil as directed on page 163, and brush the interior of the pouches with the oil.

Combine the carrots, potatoes, leek, squash, butter, oregano, and parsley in a mixing bowl. Season with salt and pepper, and toss to coat the vegetables evenly.

Divide the vegetable mixture among the pouches and top with a portion of the asparagus. Seal the pouches as described on page 163.

Arrange the pouches on the baking sheets. Bake for 10 minutes. Then reverse the position of the sheet pans in the oven, and bake for an additional 10 minutes, or until the pouches are puffed.

Remove the pouches from the oven, cut them open with scissors, taking care when opening the pouches to avoid being burned by the hot steam. Serve immediately.

Tandoori Chicken and Vegetables

Tandoori chicken is an authentic dish from the Punjab region of India and Pakistan, and gets its name from the cylindrical clay oven in which it's baked. Because the fire is at the bottom of the pot, food is exposed to live fire in addition to radiant heat and hot air convection. Serve this dish with some naan.

SERVES **4 to 6**

SIZE **13 × 18-inch half-sheet pan**

MARINATING TIME **Minimum of 4 hours**   COOKING TIME **35 to 40 minutes**

The spice mix that we know as curry powder appears to have been a British invention. Garam masala, on the other hand, is authentically Indian and its composition varies from region to region. Both curry powder and garam masala blend a number of different spices in the same way that chili powder is composed from various ingredients and marketed as a "convenience product." Garam masala has a sweeter taste than most curry powders and usually includes a mix of cinnamon, nutmeg, and cardamom, in addition to cumin, fenugreek, and fennel.

- 4 to 6 bone-in, skin-on chicken pieces of your choice (breasts cut in half, thighs, legs)
- ¾ cup plain whole-milk yogurt
- 3 tablespoons freshly squeezed lime juice
- 4 garlic cloves, smashed
- ½ small onion, diced
- 1 jalapeño or serrano chile, seeds and ribs removed
- 3 tablespoons roughly chopped fresh ginger
- 1 tablespoon tomato paste
- 1 tablespoon garam masala
- 2 teaspoons granulated sugar
- 1 teaspoon ground turmeric
- 1 teaspoon ground cumin
- 1 teaspoon paprika
- ¼ teaspoon cayenne
- Salt and freshly ground black pepper, to taste
- 3 tablespoons vegetable oil
- 2 large russet potatoes, peeled and cut into ¾-inch cubes
- 1½ pounds (½ head) cauliflower, cut into 1-inch florets
- 1 large carrot, sliced
- ¼ small red onion, thinly sliced
- ¼ cup chopped fresh cilantro, for serving

Cut deep slits in the skin of the chicken, and place it in a heavy resealable bag. Combine the yogurt, lime juice, garlic, onion, chile, ginger, tomato paste, garam masala, sugar, turmeric, cumin, paprika, cayenne, salt, and pepper in a food processor fitted with a steel blade or in a blender. Puree until smooth and scrape the mixture into the bag with the chicken pieces. Marinate the chicken in the refrigerator for a minimum of 4 hours, and up to 12 hours, turning the bag occasionally.

Preheat the oven to 425°F. Place the rack in the middle position, and line a sheet pan with heavy-duty aluminum foil. Place the oil on the pan and add the potatoes, cauliflower, and carrot. Toss the vegetables with your hands to coat them evenly and sprinkle them with salt and pepper.

Remove the chicken from the marinade, shaking it well to remove as much liquid as possible. Arrange the chicken pieces skin side down among the vegetables.

Bake the chicken and vegetables for 15 minutes. Turn over the chicken pieces with tongs and stir the vegetables. Arrange the onion slices on the top of the pan.

Bake for an additional 20 to 25 minutes, or until the chicken is cooked through and no longer pink, and the vegetables are tender. Sprinkle the dish with the cilantro and serve immediately.

NOTE The dish can be baked up to 3 hours in advance and kept at room temperature. Reheat it in a 350°F oven for 10 to 12 minutes, uncovered, or until hot.

VARIATION

∗ **Substitute 1½-inch cubes of firm, white-fleshed fish such as cod or halibut** or **large prawns** for the chicken. Marinate them for no more than 1 hour and add them to the pan after the vegetables have roasted for 20 minutes.

Chicken Fajitas

This is a mildly flavored fajita dish, although you can easily bump up the heat by adding more adobo sauce to the marinade. The vegetables and chicken share the same marinade, so the dish comes together in a unified fashion.

SERVES **4 to 6**

SIZE **2 (13 × 18-inch) half-sheet pans**

MARINATING TIME **Minimum of 20 minutes** · COOKING TIME **25 minutes**

When a marinade contains either lemon or lime juice, it's important not to marinate food longer than a recipe states because the extreme acidity in those potent liquids will acidulate foods and make them appear cooked. You really don't want chicken ceviche.

1½ **pounds boneless, skinless chicken thighs**
1 **tablespoon ground cumin**
1 **chipotle chile in adobo sauce, finely chopped**
2 **teaspoons adobo sauce, or to taste**
3 **garlic cloves, minced**
Zest and juice of 1 lime
Salt and freshly ground black pepper, to taste
⅓ **cup olive oil**
1 **large onion, halved and sliced**

1 **orange bell pepper, seeds and ribs removed, sliced**
1 **red bell pepper, seeds and ribs removed, sliced**
1 **green bell pepper, seeds and ribs removed, sliced**
4 to 6 **(10-inch) flour tortillas**
¼ **cup chopped fresh cilantro**
½ **cup grated *queso fresco*, for serving (optional)**
½ **cup fresh tomato salsa, for serving (optional)**

Cut the chicken into ¾-inch strips and place them in a heavy, resealable plastic bag. Combine the cumin, chile, adobo sauce, garlic, lime zest, lime juice, salt, and pepper in a jar with a tight-fitting lid. Shake well. Add the olive oil and shake well again. Add half of the mixture to the bag with the chicken slices and marinate the chicken for 20 minutes, turning the bag occasionally.

Preheat the oven to 400°F. Place the racks in the upper third and middle positions in the oven, and line 2 sheet pans with heavy-duty aluminum foil.

Place the onion and bell peppers in a mixing bowl and toss them with the remaining marinade. Spread the vegetables on the sheet pans. Remove the chicken from the marinade and add it to the sheet pans, discarding any remaining marinade.

Place the pans in the oven and bake for 15 minutes. Remove the pans from the oven, stir the mixture, reverse the position of the pans in the oven, and bake for 10 to 15 minutes, or until the vegetables are tender and the chicken is cooked through and no longer pink.

Wrap the tortillas in aluminum foil and place them in the oven for the last 5 minutes that the mixture cooks.

Sprinkle the cilantro over the chicken and vegetables. Spoon the mixture into the warm tortillas and serve them immediately. Pass bowls of *queso fresco* and salsa around the table, if using.

NOTE The dish can be baked up to 2 hours in advance and kept at room temperature. Reheat it in a 350°F oven for 5 to 7 minutes, or until hot.

VARIATION

* **Substitute 1½ pounds pork tenderloin** for the chicken thighs.

Middle Eastern Chicken and Couscous en Papillote

There's been a real increase in the popularity of Middle Eastern food in the past few years, so some formerly hard-to-source ingredients can now be found on supermarket shelves as well as online. One of these is za'atar, an herb and spice blend that is a utility infielder for many dishes. These pouches are colorful, with a wide range of vegetables, and are loaded with flavor.

SERVES **4 to 6**

SIZE **2 (13 × 18-inch) half-sheet pans**

TIME **20 to 25 minutes**

As with chili powder and garam masala, there are literally thousands of variations on za'atar. The history of za'atar can be traced to biblical times, and its profile is herbaceous from a combination of thyme, oregano, and frequently marjoram, along with some nuttiness from ground sesame seeds and a lemony freshness from ground sumac. If you're making a batch yourself and can't find sumac, you can substitute dried lemon zest.

- 1 **cup whole-wheat couscous**
- ¼ **cup olive oil, divided**
- 1½ **pounds boneless skinless chicken thighs**
- 4 **large shallots, thinly sliced**
- 1 **orange bell pepper, seeds and ribs discarded, thinly sliced**
- 1 **cup halved cherry or grape tomatoes**
- 2 **tablespoons za'atar**
- ½ **cup chopped fresh parsley**
- ½ **cup oil-cured black olives, chopped**
- 2 **garlic cloves, minced**
- **Salt and freshly ground black pepper, to taste**
- 1 **lemon, thinly sliced with seeds discarded**

Combine the couscous, 2 teaspoons of the oil, and 1 cup of hot tap water in a mixing bowl. Stir well, and allow the mixture to sit at room temperature for 30 minutes.

Preheat the oven to 375°F. Place the racks in the upper third and middle positions of the oven, and line 2 sheet pans with heavy-duty aluminum foil. Prepare the desired number of hearts of parchment paper or rectangles of aluminum foil as directed on page 163 and brush the interior of the pouches with 2 tablespoons of the remaining olive oil.

Cut each chicken thigh into 4 slices against the grain. Combine the chicken, remaining oil, shallots, bell pepper, tomatoes, za'atar, parsley, olives, garlic, salt, and pepper in a mixing bowl. Toss to coat the foods evenly with the seasonings.

Divide the couscous into the pouches and top with a portion of the chicken and vegetables. Lay some lemon slices on the top. Seal the pouches as described on page 163.

Arrange the pouches on the baking sheets. Bake them for 10 minutes, reverse the positions in the oven, and bake for an additional 10 to 15 minutes, or until the pouches are puffed.

Remove the pouches from the oven, cut them open with scissors, and take care to avoid being burned by the hot steam when opening the pouches. Serve immediately.

NOTE The pouches can be prepared for baking up to 1 day in advance and refrigerated. Bake them just prior to serving.

VARIATION

* **Substitute strips of chicken breast** for the chicken thighs and reduce the cooking time to a total of 18 to 20 minutes.

Pork Tenderloin with Oven-Roasted Ratatouille

A proper French ratatouille cooked on top of the stove dirties every skillet in the house because each vegetable is cooked separately and then combined with the others at the end. It's very true that the cooking times of vegetables vary, but if they're roasted in a hot oven they can be added to the sheet pans sequentially. This vividly colored and vibrantly flavored dish is perfect dinner for an early fall dinner.

SERVES **4 to 6**

SIZE **2 (13 × 18-inch) half-sheet pans**

TIME **50 minutes**

Cooking in southern France has myriad regional nuances and variations, from bouillabaisse, the famous fish stew of Marseilles, to ratatouille, a dish native to Nice, famous since the eighteenth century. Ratatouille comes from the verb *touiller*, which means "to stir up," and the noun *rata* is local slang for "chunky stew." Socca, a flat pancake made with garbanzo bean flour, is also native to Nice, and is a great bread to serve with the ratatouille.

- 1 (1½-pound) eggplant
- ½ cup kosher salt, plus additional for seasoning
- 1 large sweet onion, such as Vidalia or Bermuda, halved and cut into ½-inch slices
- 1 red bell pepper, seeds and ribs removed, cut into ½-inch slices
- 1 green bell pepper, seeds and ribs removed, cut into ½-inch slices
- 8 red-skinned potatoes, cut into ¾-inch cubes
- ⅔ cup olive oil
- 6 garlic cloves, minced
- 2 tablespoons chopped fresh rosemary
- 1 tablespoon fresh thyme leaves
- 1 (1½-pound) pork tenderloin
- 1 medium zucchini, trimmed, halved, and cut into ½-inch slices
- 1 yellow squash, trimmed, halved, and cut into ½-inch slices
- 6 ripe plum tomatoes, cored, seeded and cut into sixths
- Freshly ground black pepper, to taste
- Rosemary sprigs, for garnish (optional)

Preheat the oven to 425°F. Place the racks in the upper third and middle positions of the oven, and line 2 sheet pans with heavy-duty aluminum foil.

Discard the cap of the eggplant and cut the eggplant into 1-inch cubes. Combine ½ cup kosher salt with 1 quart cold water in a mixing bowl and add the eggplant cubes. Soak the eggplant in the salted water for 10 minutes, pressing them down into the brine with a plate. Drain the cubes and use a towel to absorb as much water as possible.

Divide the eggplant, onion, red and green bell pepper, and potatoes on the baking sheets. Mix the oil with the garlic, rosemary, and thyme. Drizzle two-thirds of the oil mixture over the vegetables and toss to coat. Rub the remaining oil on the pork tenderloin and set it aside.

Roast the vegetables for 15 minutes. Remove the pan from the oven, and add the pork, zucchini, and yellow squash. Stir to coat the vegetables, reverse the position of the pans in the oven, and roast for 10 minutes.

Add the tomatoes to the pans and season with salt and pepper. Roast for an additional 12 to 15 minutes, or until the tomatoes soften and the pork registers 140°F on an instant-read thermometer. Remove the meat from the baking sheet and allow it to rest for 5 minutes loosely covered with foil.

Carve the pork into thin slices and plate it with some of the vegetables, garnished with rosemary sprigs, if desired. Serve immediately.

NOTE The dish can be made up to 2 days in advance and refrigerated if you want to serve it at room temperature or chilled. Do not carve the pork until just before serving.

VARIATION

* **Substitute 4 to 6 chicken thigh**s for the pork tenderloin. Begin cooking them, skin side up, when the first round of vegetables goes into the oven.

Pork Saltimbocca
with Potatoes and Vegetables

Saltimbocca is typically made with veal cutlets, but I've found that pork works even better with the combination of aromatic fresh sage and salty prosciutto that are emblematic of the dish. The meat and vegetables are also treated to the combined flavors of lemon and white wine. A tossed salad with a lemon vinaigrette goes well with this dish.

SERVES **4 to 6**

SIZE **2 (13 × 18-inch) half-sheet pans**

TIME **35 minutes**

American cooks tend to think of sage as an ingredient in Thanksgiving stuffing, but this potent herb is native to the Mediterranean and is widely used in its cuisines as well. Sage is a cousin to fresh rosemary and is the best substitute for it. Add some chopped fresh sage to tomato sauce or beat it into eggs when making an omelet or frittata. Sage also enlivens cooked white beans, mixed with olive oil and garlic, as a topping for bruschetta.

- ½ cup dry white wine
- 3 tablespoons freshly squeezed lemon juice
- 3 garlic cloves, minced
- Salt and freshly ground black pepper, to taste
- ⅓ cup olive oil, divided
- 4 to 6 (6-ounce) slices of pork loin
- 1 pound Yukon Gold potatoes, cut into ½-inch slices
- 1 small fennel bulb, trimmed and cut into ½-inch slices
- 1 large onion, cut into ½-inch slices
- ¼ cup chopped fresh sage plus 8 to 12 whole sage leaves
- 8 to 12 thin slices of prosciutto

Preheat the oven to 425°F. Place the racks in the upper third and middle positions of the oven, and line 2 sheet pans with heavy-duty aluminum foil.

Combine the wine, lemon juice, garlic, salt, and pepper in a heavy resealable plastic bag and mix well to dissolve the salt. Add 3 tablespoons of the olive oil and mix well again. If necessary, pound the pork between 2 sheets of plastic wrap to a thickness of ¾ inch, using the flat side of a meat mallet or the bottom of a small skillet. Add the pork slices to the marinade and mix well. Allow the pork to marinate at room temperature while prepping the vegetables, turning the bag occasionally.

Combine the potatoes, fennel, and onion in a mixing bowl and toss with the remaining oil, salt, pepper, and chopped sage. Divide the vegetables among the sheet pans and roast for 20 minutes, or until the vegetables are beginning to brown.

Remove the pork from the marinade and pat it dry with paper towels. Place the pork on top of the vegetables and cover each piece with 2 sage leaves and 2 slices of prosciutto. Drizzle the marinade over the vegetables.

Return the sheet pans to the oven, reversing their position, and roast for 10 to 12 minutes, or until an instant-read thermometer registers 140°F when inserted into the pork. Allow the dish to cool for 5 minutes, then serve immediately.

NOTE The vegetables can be roasted up to 4 hours in advance and kept at room temperature. Do not roast the pork until just prior to serving.

Loaded Baked Potatoes

Here's a dish that pleases folks of all ages; it can be customized in myriad ways by varying the meat, cheese, and vegetables. For those of us who never met a potato we didn't like, this wintertime fare is pure heaven. A tossed salad is all you need with these spuds to call it a meal.

SERVES **4 to 6**

SIZE **13 × 18-inch half-sheet pan**

TIME **1¼ hours**

Potatoes are categorized by how they cook and the uses that are best for them; the general categories are starchy, waxy, and all-purpose. Russet potatoes are the leading contender in the starchy potato category, which is why they're great for baking and mashing. But they don't hold their shape well, which is why waxy potatoes like Red Bliss are the most popular for salads and sliced-potato dishes like gratins. My favorite all-purpose potatoes are Yukon Gold; they're great in a mash or a salad.

½ pound bacon

4 to 6 large (½ pound each) russet baking potatoes

1 cup broccoli florets, not larger than ¾-inch pieces

2 tablespoons olive oil

1 cup cherry tomatoes

4 to 6 tablespoons unsalted butter, softened

½ cup sour cream

3 tablespoons snipped fresh chives

1½ cups grated sharp cheddar cheese, divided

Salt and freshly ground black pepper, to taste

Preheat the oven to 400°F. Place the rack in the middle of the oven, and line a sheet pan with heavy-duty aluminum foil. Arrange the bacon slices on the pan and bake them for 10 minutes. Turn them over gently with tongs and bake for an additional 10 to 15 minutes, or until very crisp. Remove the bacon from the oven and drain it well on paper towels. Crumble it and set aside.

Increase the oven temperature to 425°F. Scrub the potatoes well and prick them all over with the tines of a fork. Pour off the bacon fat from the sheet pan into a low bowl, and coat the potatoes with it. Arrange the potatoes on the pan and bake them for 45 minutes.

Toss the broccoli florets with the olive oil and scatter them around the potatoes. Bake for 15 minutes. Add the cherry tomatoes to the sheet pan and bake for 5 to 10 minutes, or until they shrivel and the potatoes are tender when pierced with the tip of a paring knife.

(continued on the following page)

(continued from the previous page)

Remove the pan from the oven but leave the oven on. Cut open the potatoes and carefully scoop out the hot flesh into a mixing bowl. Add the butter, sour cream, chives, and 1 cup of the cheese. Mash with a potato masher until smooth, then add the crumbled bacon and broccoli. Mix well, season with salt and pepper, and mound the mixture back into the potato skins. Divide the tomatoes onto the top of the potatoes and then sprinkle with the remaining cheese.

Bake the potatoes again for 10 to 12 minutes, or until the cheese melts. Serve immediately.

NOTE The potatoes can be prepared up to their final baking up to 6 hours in advance and kept at room temperature.

Greek Roast Leg of Lamb

I think there's no more delicious way to complement the rosy richness of lamb than with the Greek combination of lemon, garlic, oregano, and rosemary. The same flavors also enhance the vegetables cooked with the lamb. This is a special meal for holidays or guests, which requires some advance planning, because it's really essential to marinate the meat.

SERVES **6 to 8**

SIZE **13 × 18-inch half-sheet pan**

MARINATING TIME **Minimum of 8 hours**   COOKING TIME **1 hour**

While the lemon flavor is quite dominant in this dish, a bit of lemon juice is a "secret ingredient" that can brighten the flavor of almost any dish you cook. I add some to tomato-based dishes, especially if they're made with canned tomatoes. A few drops enhance the sweetness of fresh fruit, and using it in salad dressings make them more compatible with wine.

- 1 (3- to 4-pound) boneless leg of lamb
- 6 garlic cloves, minced
- 2 tablespoons chopped fresh rosemary
- 2 tablespoons chopped fresh oregano
- 1 teaspoon grated lemon zest
- ⅓ cup freshly squeezed lemon juice
- Salt and freshly ground black pepper, to taste
- ⅓ cup olive oil
- 3 russet potatoes, peeled and cut into 1½-inch cubes or wedges
- ½ pound Brussels sprouts, trimmed and halved if large
- ½ pound baby carrots

Trim any excess fat off the leg of lamb. Combine the garlic, rosemary, oregano, lemon zest, lemon juice, salt, and pepper in a heavy resealable plastic bag. Mix well, add the olive oil, and mix well again. Place the lamb in the bag, rolling it around to coat it evenly with the marinade. Refrigerate the lamb for a minimum of 8 hours or up to 12 hours, turning the bag occasionally.

Preheat the oven to 425°F, place the rack in the middle position, and line a sheet pan with heavy-duty aluminum foil.

Remove the meat from the marinade, reserving the marinade. Cut 3 pieces of kitchen twine, about 12 inches long. Lay the twine on a platter in parallel lines. Form the meat into an oval and place it with the fat side up over the twine. Tie the meat firmly, and trim off any additional twine. Transfer the roast to the center of the pan.

(continued on the following page)

(continued from the previous page)

Roast the meat in the center of the oven for 20 minutes. Reduce the oven temperature to 400°F and place the potatoes, Brussels sprouts, and carrots around the lamb. Drizzle the reserved marinade over the vegetables.

Cook the mixture for an additional 40 to 45 minutes, or until the lamb registers 130°F for medium-rare on an instant read thermometer, or to desired doneness.

Transfer the meat to a cutting board and tent it loosely with foil. Allow it to rest for 10 minutes. Place the vegetables back in the oven and turn off the oven.

Carve the meat into thin slices and serve, drizzling the meat with any accumulated juices. Pass the vegetables around the table separately.

NOTE If this dish is not going to be served immediately, do not keep the vegetables warm. Instead reheat them in a 300°F oven for 10 minutes.

VARIATION

✳ **Substitute a 3- to 4-pound chicken** for the lamb. Marinate it the same amount of time and cook it until an instant-read thermometer registers 165°F when inserted into the thigh.

chapter 7

Roasting Pans

Unlike sheet pans, roasting pans vary greatly in size and material, and sometimes even in shape. Peculiar to the United States is an oval pan with grooves in the bottom and a high domed lid made from enameled tin, with white flecks on a black or dark blue base. While it's the right shape for a turkey or large chicken, it's virtually useless for baking lasagna for a crowd or Yorkshire pudding from the drippings of a prime rib.

While everyone has a 9 × 13 glass or porcelain pan, it's probably used more for sheet cakes than to create the centerpiece for a meal. With few exceptions, it's not large enough for all the components that are assembled for the recipes in this book.

Roasting pans are made from everything from stainless steel and aluminum to cast iron and copper, but the weight of the pan when empty should be taken into account. A cast iron roasting pan can weigh up to 25 pounds, and once a 20-pound turkey with stuffing is added, most cooks would need a forklift to retrieve it from the oven.

I'm fond of stainless steel, because it is sturdy yet light, and while a dark metal pan roasts food faster than a shiny one, it's hard to tell if the juices are nicely caramelizing or burning.

The height of the sides is important when roasting: they should be at least 3 inches high, or juices may seep out and splatter. The most useful pans are ones that measure 10 × 14 inches and 12 × 16 inches. While you can place a small amount of food in a large roasting pan, you can't jam a small pan with a large turkey.

Most roasting pans come with a rack, which allows you to elevate the food over the bottom of the pan and allows hot air to circulate for even browning. The traditional rack is V-shaped and fits snugly into the pan; a rack that folds up flat will help with storage.

While many of these recipes suggest that you line the roasting pan with heavy-duty aluminum foil, you should avoid the temptation of cooking in aluminum foil disposable pans, because they are not sturdy. Even if you place them on a cookie sheet to move them in and out of the oven, the sides can collapse.

Useful Accessories

While the rack to suspend food should be part of the roasting pan package, there are some more modern accessories that make dealing with roasting pans easier:

* A small silicone roasting rack: These are about 6 × 9 inches and about 1 inch high. They're wonderful for poultry or small pork roasts.

* Silicone bands: These are new to the market and take the place of kitchen twine to secure foods like a rolled roast. They're reusable and can withstand the heat of the grill as well as the oven.

Herb-Roasted Portobello Mushrooms

Here's a super-easy savory way to serve "meaty" portobello mushrooms as an entrée.
They're braised in beer, which, with the flavors of the herbs and garlic, becomes a delicious sauce.

SERVES **4 to 6**

SIZE **10 × 14-inch roasting pan**

TIME **20 minutes**

While portobellos should always have the stems and gills removed, don't throw them out. Clean the stems under cold running water and then add the trimmings to a stock.

NOTE The mushrooms can be roasted in advance and served at room temperature.

8 to 12 portobello mushrooms
⅓ cup olive oil
6 garlic cloves, minced
3 tablespoons chopped fresh rosemary
2 teaspoons fresh thyme leaves
Salt and freshly ground black pepper, to taste
1 cup pale ale or brown ale
4 to 6 thick slices ciabatta or other country bread
¼ cup freshly grated Parmesan cheese, for serving

Preheat the oven to 450°F, and line the roasting pan with heavy-duty aluminum foil.

Rub the mushrooms with a damp paper towel to clean them. Twist out the stems and use a small spoon to scrape out the gills; reserve for making stock. Arrange the mushrooms in the roasting pan with the gill side up.

Combine the olive oil, garlic, rosemary, thyme, salt, and pepper in a small bowl. Drizzle the mixture over the mushrooms and add the beer to the pan. Roast the mushrooms on the middle rack for 10 minutes.

Remove the pan from the oven and carefully turn the mushrooms with tongs, rolling the mushrooms in the cooking liquid. Then turn them once again so the gill side is up. Return the pan to the oven and place the bread slices on the upper rack to toast. Roast the mushrooms for an additional 10 minutes, or until the liquid is reduced and the mushrooms are caramelized.

To serve, place a slice of toast on each plate and top with 2 mushrooms. Spoon some of the sauce over them, sprinkle them with Parmesan, and serve immediately.

Vegetable Gratin

The key to the success of this vegetarian entrée, with all the sunny flavors of Provence, is to slice the vegetables thinly so that all their juices will emerge and their vibrancy comes together. Even though there's a layer of browned crumbs on top, I always serve some crusty bread alongside this dish.

SERVES **4 to 6**

SIZE **9 × 13-inch roasting pan**

TIME **1 hour**

The reason to pretreat eggplant before cooking it is to rid it of its inherent bitterness, especially if the eggplant is large. There's always some salt involved in the process, and I've found that soaking it in salt water is the most effective method. The soaking also keeps the eggplant from absorbing oil if it's going to be fried.

1 medium eggplant
½ cup kosher salt, plus additional for seasoning
½ cup olive oil, divided
1 large leek, white and pale green part, thinly sliced and well rinsed
1 small zucchini, thinly sliced
1 small yellow squash, thinly sliced
½ pound Yukon Gold potatoes, scrubbed and thinly sliced
3 large ripe beefsteak tomatoes, thinly sliced
1 tablespoon fresh thyme leaves

1 tablespoon chopped fresh rosemary
3 tablespoons chopped fresh parsley, divided
Freshly ground black pepper to taste
½ cup oil-cured black olives, pitted and chopped
¾ cup panko breadcrumbs
2 tablespoons unsalted butter, melted
⅓ cup freshly grated Parmesan cheese

Preheat the oven to 450°F and line the baking pan with heavy-duty aluminum foil.

Discard the cap of the eggplant, and cut the eggplant into ⅓-inch slices. Combine ½ cup kosher salt with 1 quart cold water in a mixing bowl, and add the eggplant slices. Soak the eggplant in the salted water for 10 minutes, pressing the slices down into the brine with a plate. Drain the slices, and use a towel to absorb as much water as possible.

Spread 2 tablespoons of the oil on the bottom of the baking pan. Place the eggplant, leek, zucchini, yellow squash, and potatoes in a mixing bowl. Spread the tomato slices on a platter.

(continued on the following page)

(continued from the previous page)

Toss the mixed vegetables with the thyme, rosemary, 1 tablespoon of the parsley, and 3 tablespoons of the oil. Sprinkle the vegetables and tomato slices with salt and pepper. Layer half the vegetables into the baking pan and cover with a layer of tomatoes. Then repeat the layering and sprinkle the olives on top. Cover the pan with foil and bake it for 20 minutes in the center of the oven.

While the vegetables bake, combine the remaining parsley, remaining oil, breadcrumbs, butter, and Parmesan in a bowl. Season with salt and pepper.

Remove the gratin from the oven and take off the foil. Press down on the vegetables with a spatula and return the pan to the oven. Bake the vegetables for 25 minutes, then sprinkle the crumb mixture on the top and bake for an additional 15 minutes, or until the crumbs are browned. Allow the gratin to sit for 5 minutes before serving.

NOTE The gratin can be assembled for baking up to 4 hours in advance. If baked in advance, it's best to serve it at room temperature rather than reheat it.

Baked Salmon with Couscous

This dish has enticing but not especially spicy flavors, so the delicacy of the fish remains the star. Sweet raisins balance the mild heat from the spices, and a hearty sprinkling of toasted almonds at the end adds some textural diversity.

SERVES **4 to 6**

SIZE **10 × 14-inch roasting pan**

TIME **25 minutes**

Contrary to popular belief, couscous is not a grain. It's a finely milled form of pasta made from semolina wheat, which means it is not part of a gluten-free diet. But unlike the difference in cooking times of white rice and brown rice, both whole wheat couscous, which contains some of the endosperm and bran, and white couscous cook in the same short amount of time. So feel free to substitute one for the other.

NOTE The dish should be cooked just prior to serving, or it can be served cold.

VARIATION

* **Cod, halibut, or sea bass can be substituted** for the salmon.

½ cup slivered blanched almonds
1½ cups couscous
2 carrots, thinly sliced
2 ripe plum tomatoes, cored, seeded, and diced
1 garlic clove, minced
1 shallot, finely chopped
½ cup raisins, preferably golden
½ cup dry white wine
½ cup freshly squeezed orange juice
½ cup Seafood Stock (page 32) or store-bought stock
2 tablespoons olive oil
2 teaspoons harissa
2 teaspoons ground cumin
2 teaspoons sweet paprika
1 teaspoon ground coriander
4 to 6 (5- to 6-ounce) skinless salmon fillets, about ¾-inch thick
½ lemon, thinly sliced with seeds discarded
Salt and freshly ground black pepper, to taste
2 tablespoons chopped fresh cilantro, for serving

Preheat the oven to 375°F and line the roasting pan with heavy-duty aluminum foil. Toast the almonds for 5 minutes, or until lightly browned. Remove the almonds from the baking pan and set them aside. Increase the oven temperature to 450°F.

Combine the couscous, carrots, tomatoes, garlic, shallot, raisins, wine, orange juice, stock, oil, harissa, cumin, paprika, and coriander in the baking pan. Add ⅔ cup of water, and stir well. Place the salmon fillets on top of the couscous and top each with a lemon slice. Season the fish and couscous mixture with salt and pepper.

Cover the baking pan tightly with foil and bake for 20 minutes, or until the salmon is opaque and the liquid has been absorbed.

To serve, transfer the salmon to plates and fluff the couscous with a fork. Place the couscous next to the salmon and sprinkle the toasted almonds over the couscous and the cilantro over the salmon. Serve immediately.

New Wave Fish and Chips

Fish and chips don't have to be fried, as you'll find out when you make this dish. The combination of baking and broiling gives you perfectly crispy potatoes, and the marinated fish is succulent. A tossed salad makes a complete meal.

SERVES **4 to 6**

SIZE **10 × 14-inch metal roasting pan**

TIME **50 minutes**

> When cooking fish conventionally, the 10-Minute Rule or Canadian Cooking Method is a good guideline. It was developed by the Canadian Department of Fisheries to try to boost consumption of fish in their country. While not perfect, it certainly makes for an easy rule of thumb: cook fish for a total of 10 minutes per inch of thickness.

Vegetable oil spray

1½ pounds large redskin potatoes, thinly sliced

4 shallots, thinly sliced

½ cup olive oil, divided

3 garlic cloves, minced, divided

3 tablespoons snipped fresh chives

Salt and freshly ground black pepper, to taste

1½ pounds halibut fillet, about ¾-inch thick, cut into 4 to 6 even-sized pieces

3 tablespoons dry white wine

2 tablespoons freshly squeezed lemon juice

2 tablespoons chopped fresh parsley

2 teaspoons fresh thyme leaves

2 teaspoons grated lemon zest

Place the oven rack so that it is 4 to 6 inches from the broiler element and preheat the oven to 400°F. Line the roasting pan with heavy-duty aluminum foil and spray the foil with vegetable oil spray.

Combine the potatoes, shallots, ¼ cup of the olive oil, 1 garlic clove, chives, salt, and pepper in a mixing bowl. Toss well to coat the vegetables evenly. Arrange the potatoes in the prepared pan and bake them for 40 minutes, or until they have softened and are beginning to brown.

While the potatoes bake, combine the remaining oil, remaining garlic, fish pieces, wine, lemon juice, parsley, thyme, lemon zest, and additional salt and pepper in a heavy resealable plastic bag. Allow the fish to marinate at room temperature while the potatoes bake, turning the bag occasionally.

Remove the potatoes from the oven and preheat the oven broiler. Using a spatula, move the potatoes around so they become 4 to 6 mounds rather than spread out in the roasting pan.

Remove the fish from the marinade and discard the marinade. Arrange the fish portions over the potatoes. Broil the fish for 5 to 8 minutes, or until cooked to desired doneness. Allow the dish to sit for 5 minutes, and then serve.

NOTE The potatoes can be baked up to 4 hours in advance and kept at room temperature. Do not broil the fish until just prior to serving.

VARIATION

∗ **You can substitute cod, salmon, arctic char**, or any thick fish fillet for the halibut.

Steamed Mussels Provençal

A tossed salad and a loaf of crusty bread are all you need to enjoy every drop of the aromatic and flavorful broth in this meal. Using a roasting pan in the hot oven means that all the mussels steam open at the same time, unlike when cooking them on top of the stove.

SERVES **4 to 6**

SIZE **12 × 16-inch metal roasting pan**

TIME **20 minutes**

Almost all of the mussels we eat are farmed, which is why I no longer include directions for scraping off the beard; that only matters with harvested mussels. Should you find one with a beard, just pull it off using a clean dish towel. There are two main species of mussels in North America. The most common is the blue mussel (*Mytilus edulis*), farmed in the Atlantic, which is at its peak in fall and winter. The Mediterranean mussel (*Mytilus galloprovincialis*), which comes from the Pacific or Europe, is slightly larger; its peak season is spring and summer. Between these two species, fresh mussels are always available.

4 to 6 pounds fresh mussels
1 juice orange
2 tablespoons olive oil
½ small red onion, diced
½ small fennel bulb, diced
1 red bell pepper, seeds and ribs removed, chopped
4 garlic cloves, minced
1 (14.5-ounce) can diced tomatoes, undrained
½ cup dry white wine

2 tablespoons chopped fresh parsley
2 tablespoons chopped fresh tarragon
1 tablespoon fresh thyme leaves
2 bay leaves
2 tablespoons unsalted butter, cut into small pieces
Salt and freshly ground black pepper, to taste
4 to 6 (1-inch-thick) slices hearty bread, toasted, for serving

Place the oven rack in the lowest position and preheat the oven to 500°F.

Scrub the mussels under cold running water, scraping off any beards, if necessary. Grate the zest from the orange and squeeze the juice from the orange. Set aside.

Heat the oil in the roasting pan over medium-high heat. Add the onion, fennel, and red bell pepper and cook, stirring occasionally, for 3 minutes, or until the onion is translucent. Add the garlic and cook for 1 minute.

Add the orange juice, orange zest, tomatoes, wine, parsley, tarragon, thyme, and bay leaves to the pan and bring to a boil over medium-high heat. Boil for 1 minute. Add the mussels to the pan, and cover the pan tightly with heavy-duty aluminum foil.

Place the pan in the oven and cook for 15 to 18 minutes, or until the mussels have steamed open. Remove the pan from the oven, remove and discard the bay leaves, and stir in the butter. Season with salt and pepper, and serve immediately in low bowls over the toast slices.

NOTE The mussel base can be made up to 4 hours in advance and kept at room temperature. Bring it to a boil before adding the mussels.

VARIATION

* **Substitute littleneck clams** for the mussels.

Middle Eastern Chicken
with Garbanzo Beans

*With the increase in interest in the cuisines of the Middle East and North Africa, sumac has
wended its way into many American kitchens. In this dish the rosy color of the sumac is echoed
by the orange carrots, and you'll find that garbanzo beans become crunchy when roasted.
In fact, I frequently roast additional garbanzo beans so I'll have them to snack on.*

SERVES **4 to 6**

SIZE **12 × 16-inch roasting pan**

TIME **½ to 2 hours**

The sumac bush is native to the Middle East and to Sicily, and is a distant cousin of that weed in the backyard that caused a rash when you were a kid. It has a tangy, lemony flavor, and the powder ground from its deep red berries gives all foods a real pop of color. I've sprinkled it directly on cantaloupe and other melons, and when combined with tangy blood orange juice, olive oil, and garlic, it becomes a great marinade.

1 (3½- to 4-pound) whole chicken
2 tablespoons ground sumac
1 teaspoon ground cumin
1 teaspoon ground coriander
½ teaspoon crushed red pepper flakes
Salt and freshly ground black pepper, to taste
1 lemon, divided

3 garlic cloves, minced
⅓ cup olive oil, divided
1 pound baby carrots
2 (15-ounce) cans garbanzo beans, drained and rinsed
1 tablespoon honey
2 tablespoons dry white wine
1 tablespoon sweet paprika
½ cup chopped fresh cilantro, for serving

Preheat the oven to 400°F and line the roasting pan with heavy-duty aluminum foil. Place a 6 × 9-inch silicone roasting rack on top of the foil.

Pat the chicken dry with paper towels and place it on the rack. Combine the sumac, cumin, coriander, crushed red pepper flakes, salt, and pepper in a small bowl, and mix well. Squeeze the juice of half of the lemon into the spices, and stir in the garlic and 2 tablespoons of the oil. Mix well and rub the paste all over the outside and inside of the chicken. Cut the squeezed lemon half into pieces and insert them inside the chicken.

Place the carrots and garbanzo beans in a mixing bowl. Combine the honey, wine, paprika, salt, and pepper in a small bowl, and stir well. Add the remaining oil, and then toss the liquid with the vegetables. Spread the vegetables around the chicken. Cut the remaining half lemon into slices and place them on top of the vegetables.

Roast the chicken for 1½ to 2 hours, rotating the pan after 1 hour, or until an instant-read thermometer registers 165°F when inserted into the thigh. Remove the chicken from the oven, tent it loosely with foil, and allow it to rest for 10 minutes before carving. Plate the vegetables next to the chicken, and sprinkle some cilantro on each serving.

NOTE The chicken can be prepared for roasting up to 3 hours in advance and refrigerated, tightly covered.

Herbed Roast Chicken
with Sausage Sage Stuffing

Stuffing need not be confined to turkeys on Thanksgiving, and this chicken cooked with herbed stuffing makes any meal feel like a holiday. It contains the distinctive flavor of sage, and the croutons in the stuffing brown as the chicken cooks.

SERVES 4 to 6

SIZE 12 × 16-inch metal roasting pan

TIME 1½ hours

Cremini mushrooms are merely portobello mushrooms that are small and young, and baby bella is just a name under which some cremini mushrooms are marketed. The dark gills are exposed because the portobello mushrooms are allowed to ripen after being picked. The appeal of these mushrooms is that they have much more inherent flavor than white button mushrooms.

6 tablespoons (¾ stick) unsalted butter, softened, divided
6 ounces bulk pork or poultry sausage
1 large onion, diced
2 celery ribs, diced
½ fennel bulb, diced
¼ pound cremini mushrooms, diced
2 garlic cloves, minced
⅓ cup chopped fresh sage, divided

2 tablespoons fresh thyme leaves, divided
1¼ cups Chicken Stock (page 30) or store-bought stock, divided
1 (4- to 4½-pound) chicken, giblets removed
Salt and freshly ground black pepper, to taste
4 cups firmly packed ¾-inch cubes of ciabatta or other hearty white bread

Preheat the oven to 425°F.

Place the roasting pan on the top of the stove, preferably over two burners. Heat 2 tablespoons of the butter over medium heat. Crumble the sausage into the pan, breaking up lumps with a fork. Cook, stirring frequently, until the sausage loses its pink color.

Add the onion, celery, fennel, and mushrooms to the pan. Cook, stirring frequently, for 3 minutes. Add the garlic, 2 tablespoons of the sage, and 2 teaspoons of the thyme and cook for 1 minute, or until the onions soften. Add ¼ cup of the stock to the pan and cook for 2 minutes over medium-high heat, or until it almost evaporates.

(continued on the following page)

(continued from the previous page)

Combine the remaining butter, remaining sage, remaining thyme, salt, and pepper in a small bowl and mix well. Carefully lift the skin on the breast of the chicken and insert the herbed butter mixture. Season the cavity of the chicken with salt and pepper.

Push the vegetables to the sides of the roasting pan and place a 6 × 9-inch silicone roasting rack in the center. Place the chicken on top of the rack, breast side down. Spread out the vegetables and then top them with the bread cubes.

Roast the chicken in the center of the oven for 30 minutes. Gently turn it breast side up and roast for an additional 40 to 50 minutes, or until an instant-read thermometer registers 165°F when inserted into the thigh.

Transfer the chicken to a carving board, cover it loosely with foil, and allow it to rest for 15 minutes. Remove the roasting rack from the pan, and stir the stuffing. Sprinkle the remaining stock over the stuffing, cover the pan with foil, and allow it to sit for 10 minutes to moisten. Use additional stock or water if the stuffing seems dry.

To serve, carve the chicken and serve it along with the stuffing.

NOTE The chicken and stuffing can be prepared 1 day in advance and refrigerated separately, tightly covered. Reheat the stuffing wrapped in heavy-duty aluminum foil and the chicken carved into slices in a pan covered with foil in a 350°F oven for 10 to 15 minutes, or until hot.

VARIATION

٭ **The nature of the dish changes with the type of bread used.** If you use an herb or olive bread, it will add another dimension of flavor to the dish, as will varying the type of sausage used.

Curried Chicken with Lentils

This is not an overly spicy dish, but the turmeric and ginger give it a vibrant flavor. In keeping with the Indian nature of the ingredients, I usually serve it with warmed naan bread on the side.

SERVES **4 to 6**

SIZE **10 × 14-inch roasting pan**

TIME **50 minutes**

Lentils are a small, flat, round seed that is one of the fastest to cook when dried, so they don't require any presoaking. Lentils come in a variety of colors, each of which has a slightly different cooking time. They also come split, as well as whole. Split lentils cook in merely a few minutes and are great if you plan to puree them.

NOTE The lentils can be partially baked up to 6 hours in advance and kept at room temperature. Reheat them, covered with foil, before finishing the dish.

VARIATION

* **Substitute 1 pound of firm, white-fleshed fish fillets like cod** for the chicken and **substitute seafood stock** for the chicken stock. Bake the lentils for 30 minutes before topping them with the fish, and then only bake the fish for 10 minutes.

1 large onion, diced
2 tablespoons minced fresh ginger
2 tablespoons olive oil
1½ cups dried red lentils (not split lentils)
1 (15-ounce) can light coconut milk
1½ cups Chicken Stock (page 30) or store-bought stock
2 teaspoons ground turmeric, divided
1¼ pounds boneless, skinless chicken thighs
¼ cup plain yogurt
1 tablespoon garam masala
Salt and freshly ground black pepper, to taste
3 ripe plum tomatoes, cored, seeded, and diced
¼ cup chopped fresh cilantro, for serving
Lime wedges, for serving

Preheat the oven to 400°F and line the roasting pan with heavy-duty aluminum foil.

Combine the onion, ginger, and oil in the roasting pan and mix to coat the onions. Roast the onions for 10 minutes.

While the onions roast, rinse the lentils well in a sieve under cold running water. Add the lentils to the roasting pan and stir in the coconut milk, stock, and 1½ teaspoons of the turmeric. Cover the pan with foil and bake the lentils for 15 minutes.

While the lentils bake, pat the chicken dry with paper towels. Combine the yogurt, garam masala, remaining turmeric, salt, and pepper in small bowl, and stir well. Spread the mixture on both sides of the chicken pieces.

Remove the lentils from the oven, stir in the tomatoes, and season with salt and pepper. Place the chicken on top of the lentils and bake for 25 minutes, or until the chicken is cooked through and no longer pink. Serve immediately, sprinkling each serving with cilantro and passing lime wedges.

Tarragon Game Hens
with Fennel and Potatoes

In this dish, the juices from the butterflied Cornish game hens provide the flavorful sauce for the fennel and potatoes that are cooked with them in the roasting pan. The combination of anise-scented tarragon, heady garlic, and fresh lemon zest perfectly complements all three ingredients.

SERVES **4 to 6**

SIZE **12 × 16-inch baking pan**

TIME **1 hour**

While the stalks of fennel left attached to the bulbs are rarely used in recipes, you can use it in place of celery ribs when making a batch of tuna or chicken salad, or as a crunchy addition to a tossed green salad. The colorful fronds create a dramatic garnish for soups, too.

NOTE The dish can be prepared up to 1 day in advance and refrigerated, tightly covered. Reheat it, covered with foil, in a 325°F oven for 15 to 20 minutes, or until hot.

- 2 or 3 (1¾-pound) Cornish game hens
- 4 tablespoons (½ stick) unsalted butter, softened
- ¼ cup chopped fresh tarragon leaves
- 4 garlic cloves, minced
- 2 teaspoons grated lemon zest
- Kosher salt and freshly ground black pepper, to taste
- 2 small fennel bulbs (about 1¼ pounds total)
- 2 or 3 russet potatoes, peeled and cut into 1-inch cubes

Preheat the oven to 425°F. Place the rack in the middle position of the oven, and line a roasting pan with heavy-duty aluminum foil.

Using poultry shears or a sharp knife, cut along the backs of the hens. Turn them over and press them flat with the palm of your hand. Mix the butter, tarragon, garlic, lemon zest, salt, and pepper in a small bowl. Lift the skin around the breasts of the hens and divide the seasoned butter between them. Sprinkle both sides of the hens with salt and pepper and arrange them in the pan. Bake the hens for 30 minutes, with the skin side up.

Remove the stalks from the fennel bulbs, and trim off the bottom. Cut each bulb into 6 segments, keeping the core whole so that each section retains its shape. Remove the hens from the oven and remove them with tongs from the roasting pan. Arrange the fennel segments with the cut sides down and the potato cubes in the pan and place the hens on top of them. Baste the hens with the juices that have accumulated in the pan.

Return the pan to the oven and roast the vegetables for 15 minutes. Turn over the fennel segments and potato cubes with tongs and roast for an additional 15 minutes, or until the vegetables are tender and the hens register 165°F on an instant-read thermometer inserted into the thighs.

To serve, cut the hens in half and plate each half with some of the vegetables, spooning the juices over the top.

VARIATION

* **Substitute 2 (2- to 3-pound) chickens** for the Cornish game hens, and bake them for 1¼ to 1½ hours, or until the thigh meat registers 165°F on an instant-read thermometer.

Herbed Roasted Pork with Vegetable Hash

Roasting vegetables in a hot oven has become the common wisdom for the past few years, but it is akin to incinerating them much of the time. Vegetables are full of wonderful natural sugars that emerge during a long time in a relatively cool oven. The same low temperature is a friend to such inexpensive cuts as pork butt, and when roasted together with vegetables, it makes a fantastic dinner.

SERVES **4 to 6**

SIZE **10 × 14-inch roasting pan**

MARINATING TIME **Minimum of 4 hours**

COOKING TIME **2 hours**

If you have leftovers from a one-pan dinner, it's good to think about how you'll utilize them before refrigerating them. In this case any leftover pork would make great sandwiches, so it makes sense to thinly slice the whole roast and refrigerate the meat separately. The leftover vegetables can be reheated in a 300°F oven for 10 to 15 minutes, or until hot.

PORK

- 1 (2-pound) boneless pork butt roast, rolled and tied
- 2 tablespoons Dijon mustard
- 3 garlic cloves, minced
- ¼ cup chopped fresh sage
- 1 tablespoon fresh thyme leaves
- Kosher salt and freshly ground black pepper, to taste

VEGETABLE HASH

- 4 parsnips
- 4 carrots
- 4 russet potatoes
- 1 large onion, diced
- 12 whole garlic cloves, unpeeled
- ⅓ cup olive oil
- 1 tablespoon chopped fresh sage
- 2 teaspoons fresh thyme leaves
- Kosher salt and freshly ground black pepper, to taste

Place the pork roast on a cutting board. Combine the mustard, garlic, sage, thyme, salt, and pepper in a small bowl and mix well. Use a boning knife to create a hole in the center of the roast, and insert half the herb mixture into it. Rub the remaining mixture on the surface of the pork. Wrap the pork tightly with plastic wrap and refrigerate it for a minimum of 4 hours, or up to 24 hours. Allow the roast to sit at room temperature for 1 hour before roasting it.

Preheat the oven to 325°F, and line a roasting pan with heavy-duty aluminum foil.

Peel the parsnips, carrots, and potatoes, and cut them into 1-inch cubes. Place them in the roasting pan and add the diced onion and garlic cloves. Drizzle with the olive oil, and then toss the mixture with the sage, thyme, salt, and pepper.

Make room for the pork roast in the center of the pan, and roast the meat with the fat side up for a total of 1½ to 2 hours, or until an instant-read thermometer registers 155°F in the center of the pork. Stir the vegetables every 30 minutes so they brown evenly.

Remove the pork from the oven, transfer it to platter, cover it loosely with aluminum foil, and allow it to rest for 20 minutes. Return the vegetables to the oven, turn off the oven, and allow them to remain hot.

To serve, thinly slice the meat against the grain, sprinkling it with any juices that have accumulated, and plate it with a serving of the vegetable hash.

NOTE The dish can be roasted up to 3 hours in advance and kept at room temperature. Slice the pork while it's cool and reheat the whole dish at 325°F for 10 minutes before serving.

Italian Sausages with Grapes and Polenta

Sweet and savory is a timeless combination, which is why slices of prosciutto go so well with succulent figs and cubes of melon. In this case the pairing is seedless grapes and sausage. This dish is also a great way to take advantage of those tubes of precooked polenta you see in the supermarket. The polenta nicely picks up all the nuanced sweet and spicy flavors of the sausages and grapes.

SERVES **4 to 6**

SIZE **10 × 14-inch roasting pan**

TIME **1 hour to 70 minutes**

To me, sausage is the ultimate convenience food, because someone has already spent the time to chop up protein and—with any luck—has skillfully seasoned it. All the cook must do is cook or reheat it. Today, so many formulations are also made with poultry, so for anyone who is cutting back on red meat, there's a multitude of options.

NOTE The dish can be prepared for baking up to 2 days in advance and refrigerated, tightly covered with plastic wrap. Do not bake it or drizzle it with vinegar until just prior to serving.

VARIATION

＊ **Substitute 1 pound of red potatoes,** scrubbed and cut into ¾-inch cubes, for the polenta.

Vegetable oil spray
1 (1-pound) tube precooked polenta
1½ pounds links of uncooked sweet or spicy Italian sausage, either pork or poultry sausage
¾ pound red seedless grapes
¾ pound green seedless grapes
2 leeks, white and light green parts, cut into ½-inch slices and rinsed well
2 tablespoons chopped fresh parsley
2 tablespoons chopped fresh oregano
1 tablespoon chopped fresh basil
3 tablespoons olive oil
2 tablespoons sherry vinegar
Salt and freshly ground black pepper, to taste

Preheat the oven to 350°F and line the roasting pan with heavy-duty aluminum foil. Spray the foil with vegetable oil spray.

Cut the polenta into ¾-inch slices and arrange them on the bottom of the baking dish. Prick the sausages all over with the tines of a sharp fork, and arrange the links in the pan on top of the polenta.

Combine the red grapes, green grapes, leeks, parsley, oregano, basil, and olive oil in a mixing bowl and toss well. Place the mixture on top of the sausages and polenta.

Bake the dish, uncovered, in the center of the oven for 1 hour to 70 minutes, or until the sausages are cooked through; the amount of time depends on the diameter of the sausage links. Drizzle the vinegar over the dish, season with salt and pepper, and serve immediately.

Gratin of Veal
with Wild Mushrooms

This is a classic French dish that is worthy of the most elegant dinner party, but it's also extremely easy to assemble. After using your baking dish as a skillet to cook a combination of onions and shiitake mushrooms, you simply layer on the veal and some cheesy crumbs, pour liquid over the whole thing, and bake it. I usually serve this gratin with a tossed salad or some chilled asparagus.

SERVES **4 to 6**

SIZE **9 × 13-inch metal roasting pan**

TIME **1¼ hours**

It's only been in the past decade that most of us have been introduced to the wonders of fresh shiitake mushrooms. Native to Asia, they've been part of Chinese restaurant food forever, but only in their dried form. With the advent of large-scale wild mushroom cultivation in the United States, we can now find them just about everywhere, and the prices appear to have stabilized and even reduced slightly. Unlike button mushrooms, shiitakes actually have some nutritional value, including many B vitamins.

1½ pounds veal scallops
Salt and freshly ground black pepper, to taste
3 tablespoons unsalted butter
3 large onions, diced
½ pound fresh shiitake mushrooms, stemmed and sliced
1 tablespoon fresh thyme leaves

1½ cups panko breadcrumbs
1½ cups grated Gruyère cheese, divided
1½ cups Chicken Stock (page 30) or store-bought stock
1 cup dry white wine

Preheat the oven to 350°F. Pound the veal scallops between 2 sheets of plastic wrap to an even thickness of ¼ inch. Season the veal scallops with salt and pepper, and set aside.

Melt the butter in the roasting pan over medium heat. Add the onions and stir to coat them well. Cook the onions for 7 minutes. Add the mushrooms, increase the heat to medium-high, and sprinkle with salt and pepper. Cook for an additional 2 minutes, or until the onions are soft and the mushrooms have wilted. Stir in the thyme and cook for 30 seconds. Remove the roasting pan from the heat.

Mix the breadcrumbs with 1 cup of the cheese. Sprinkle half of the mixture on top of the onions and mushrooms. Place overlapping veal slices on top of the crumbs. Firmly press the remaining cheese mixture into the veal with a spatula. Sprinkle the remaining cheese on top, and pour the chicken stock and white wine over all.

Cover the pan with aluminum foil, and bake for 30 minutes. Remove the foil and bake for an additional 45 minutes, or until the top is browned and the veal is fork-tender. Cut the gratin into sections and remove them from the pan with a spatula. Serve immediately.

NOTE The dish can be assembled up to 1 day in advance and refrigerated, tightly covered. Add 10 minutes to the initial baking time if the dish is chilled.

VARIATION

* **Substitute pieces of pork tenderloin** pounded to a thickness of ¼ inch for the veal scallops.

Roasted Spiced Beef
with Sweet Potatoes and Parsnips

*The vibrant cuisines of North Africa are the inspiration for this
Sunday-meat-and-potatoes family-pleasing dinner. Any leftover beef makes
superb sandwiches for lunch the next day. Serve this dish with a
crisp tossed salad.*

SERVES **4 to 6**

SIZE **10 × 14-inch metal roasting pan**

TIME **1½ hours**

Eye of round roast is an underutilized cut of beef. It's as lean as a tenderloin, but has a tendency to dry out if cooked at a high temperature. It should always be roasted at 350°F and must rest before being carved.

2 or 3 medium sweet potatoes, peeled and cut into 1-inch chunks
6 parsnips, cut on the diagonal into 1½-inch pieces
3 tablespoons olive oil
2 tablespoons harissa, or to taste
Salt and freshly ground black pepper, to taste
2 tablespoons fresh thyme leaves
1 tablespoon chopped fresh oregano

2 teaspoons ground sumac
2 tablespoons sesame seeds
2 teaspoons ground cumin
2 teaspoons ground coriander
½ teaspoon ground ginger
1 (2½- to 3-pound) eye of round roast
3 garlic cloves, cut into quarters lengthwise
2 tablespoons toasted sesame oil

Preheat the oven to 350°F and line the roasting pan with heavy-duty aluminum foil.

Place the sweet potatoes and parsnips in the pan. Combine the olive oil, harissa, salt, and pepper in a small bowl and stir well. Toss the vegetables with the mixture and roast them in the center of the oven for 30 minutes.

Combine the thyme, oregano, sumac, sesame seeds, cumin, coriander, ginger, salt, and pepper in a bowl and mix well. Cut slits in the meat with the tip of a paring knife and insert a quarter of garlic in each. Rub the roast with the sesame oil and then rub it all over with the spice mixture.

Make space in the center of the roasting pan for the meat and return the pan to the oven. Bake for 45 minutes, or until an instant-read thermometer registers 125°F for medium-rare or to desired doneness. Transfer the meat to a carving board and tent it loosely with aluminum foil. Allow it to rest for 10 minutes.

Increase the oven temperature to 450°F. Spread the vegetables in an even layer and roast them for 10 minutes, or until browned.

Slice the meat thinly and serve it alongside the vegetables.

NOTE The first 30 minutes of roasting the vegetables can be done up to 4 hours in advance. Do not cook the meat or brown the vegetables until just prior to serving.

Reuben Sandwich Casserole with Sauerkraut and Swiss Cheese

Assembling sandwiches for a crowd can be tedious, but taking all the components of a traditional Reuben sandwich and transforming them into a casserole is both easy and delicious. The key is to make your own Thousand Island dressing, and I suggest making a large batch and using the remainder on salads.

SERVES **4 to 6**

SIZE **9 × 13-inch roasting pan**

TIME **35 minutes**

Although it is now defunct, Reuben's Delicatessen was a New York institution that opened in the late 1890s. Legend has it that owner Arthur Reuben invented the Reuben sandwich there in 1914 for the cast of a Charlie Chaplin film. It contains sauerkraut, corned beef, Swiss cheese, and Russian dressing, and it's served grilled on seeded rye bread.

DRESSING
- 1 hard-cooked egg yolk
- 1 small shallot, finely chopped
- 1 garlic clove, pushed through a garlic press
- 1¼ cups mayonnaise, homemade or your favorite commercial
- 2 tablespoons ketchup
- 2 tablespoons bottled chili sauce
- 2 tablespoons sweet pickle relish
- 1 teaspoon cider vinegar
- ¼ teaspoon hot red pepper sauce, or to taste

CASSEROLE
- 1 (2-pound) package sauerkraut
- 2 teaspoons caraway seeds
- 3 cups shredded Swiss cheese
- 1 pound thinly sliced cooked corned beef, coarsely chopped
- 6 slices seeded rye bread, cut horizontally into 1-inch strips
- 3 tablespoons unsalted butter, melted

Preheat the oven to 375°F and grease the roasting pan.

For the dressing, press the egg yolk through a fine mesh sieve into a mixing bowl. Add the shallot, garlic, mayonnaise, ketchup, chili sauce, pickle relish, vinegar, and hot red pepper sauce to the bowl. Whisk until well blended. Set aside.

Place the sauerkraut in a colander and press with the back of a spoon to extract as much liquid as possible. Rinse the sauerkraut under cold running water for 2 minutes. Then place the sauerkraut in a large mixing bowl and fill the bowl with cold water. Soak the sauerkraut for 5 minutes. Drain the sauerkraut in a colander again, pressing with the back of a spoon to extract as much liquid as possible. Place the sauerkraut in the prepared baking pan and sprinkle it with the caraway seeds.

Add half of the Swiss cheese, half of the dressing, and half of the corned beef in an even layer, then repeat with the remaining ingredients. Brush one side of the bread strips with the melted butter, and place them with the buttered side up on top of the dish.

Cover the pan with aluminum foil and bake for 10 minutes. Remove the foil, and bake for an additional 25 minutes, or until the bread is browned and the casserole is bubbling. Serve immediately.

NOTE Up to topping dish with the buttered bread, the casserole can be assembled up to 2 days in advance and refrigerated, tightly covered. Add 10 minutes to the covered baking time if it's chilled.

METRIC CONVERSION CHARTS

The recipes that appear in this cookbook use the standard United States method for measuring liquid and dry or solid ingredients (teaspoons, tablespoons, and cups). The information on this chart is provided to help cooks outside the U.S. successfully use these recipes. All equivalents are approximate.

METRIC EQUIVALENTS FOR DIFFERENT TYPES OF INGREDIENTS

STANDARD CUP	FINE POWDER (e.g. flour)	GRAIN (e.g. rice)	GRANULAR (e.g. sugar)	LIQUID SOLIDS (e.g. butter)	LIQUID (e.g. milk)
¾	105 g	113 g	143 g	150 g	180 ml
⅔	93 g	100 g	125 g	133 g	160 ml
½	70 g	75 g	95 g	100 g	120 ml
⅓	47 g	50 g	63 g	67 g	80 ml
¼	35 g	38 g	48 g	50 g	60 ml
⅛	18 g	19 g	24 g	25 g	30 ml

USEFUL EQUIVALENTS FOR LIQUID INGREDIENTS BY VOLUME

¼ tsp	=						1 ml
½ tsp	=						2 ml
1 tsp	=						5 ml
3 tsp	=	1 tbls	=		½ fl oz	=	15 ml
		2 tbls	=	⅛ cup	1 fl oz	=	30 ml
		4 tbls	=	¼ cup	2 fl oz	=	60 ml
		5⅓ tbls	=	⅓ cup	3 fl oz	=	80 ml
		8 tbls	=	½ cup	4 fl oz	=	120 ml
		10⅔ tbls	=	⅔ cup	5 fl oz	=	160 ml
		12 tbls	=	¾ cup	6 fl oz	=	180 ml
		16 tbls	=	1 cup	8 fl oz	=	240 ml
		1 pt	=	2 cups	16 fl oz	=	480 ml
		1 qt	=	4 cups	32 fl oz	=	960 ml
					33 fl oz	=	1000 ml = 1 L

USEFUL EQUIVALENTS FOR DRY INGREDIENTS BY WEIGHT

(To convert ounces to grams, multiply the number of ounces by 28.35.)

1 oz	=	¹⁄₁₆ lb	=	28.3 g
4 oz	=	¼ lb	=	113 g
8 oz	=	½ lb	=	227 g
12 oz	=	¾ lb	=	340 g
16 oz	=	1 lb	=	454 g

ACKNOWLEDGMENTS

It not only takes a village to raise a child, it certainly takes a large one to bring a cookbook to fruition. My thanks go:

To Jennifer Williams, my editor at Sterling Epicure, for all her wisdom, belief in this idea, and guidance.

To Chris Bain, photo director at Sterling, for his vision, and to production editor Scott Amerman who kept the project on track.

To cover designer Jo Obarowski and interior designer Christine Heun whose work makes this book visually sing.

To Bill Milne for his inspired photography and use of his seemingly unending series of great props.

To Diane Vezza, whose talented food styling makes these photographs so appealing and is such a delight to work with.

To Julianna Vezza, Diane's very talented daughter, and Terry Greico Kenny, who both provided countless hours of kitchen assistance.

To Ed Claflin, my agent, for his constant support, encouragement, and humor.

To my dear family for their love and support, especially to Nancy and Walter Dubler; Ariela Dubler; Jesse Furman; Ilan, Mira, and Lev Dubler-Furman; Joshua Dubler; Lisa Cerami; Zahir and Charlie Cerami; and to David Krimm and Peter Bradley.

To my many friends who critiqued my work as any number of dishes emerged from three pressure cookers every day, especially to Constance Brown, Kenn Speiser, Karen Davidson, Fox Wetle, Richard Besdine, Vicki Veh, Joe Chazan, Kim Montour, Nick Brown, Bruce Tillinghast, Edye de Marco, Sylvia Brown, Andrew West, and Bob Oates.

And to Patches and Rufous, my beloved feline companions, who kept me company in between their naps and served as inspiration for all of the fish and seafood recipes.

INDEX

ABOUT THE AUTHOR

photo by Constance Brown

ELLEN BROWN gained the national limelight in 1982, as the founding food editor of *USA Today*. She is the author of more than forty cookbooks, ranging from topics as varied as sushi to smoothies and fondue to fajitas. Her bestselling book, *The New Cast Iron Skillet Cookbook*, was published by Sterling Epicure in 2014, and it was followed in 2016 by *The New Pressure Cooker Cookbook*. Brown has written for the *Providence Journal* for more than a decade, and her articles have appeared in more than two dozen publications, including *The Washington Post*, *The Los Angeles Times*, *Bon Appetit*, and *Art Culinaire*. In 1985, she was inducted into the prestigious Who's Who of Cooking in America. Profiles of her have appeared in *The Washington Post*, *The Detroit News*, *Coastal Living*, *The Providence Journal*, and *The Miami Herald*. Her cooking on Nantucket, where she owned a catering service, was the subject of an episode on *Food Finds*, shown nationally on the Television Food Network. She lives in Providence, Rhode Island.